Studies in English and American Literature, Linguistics,
and Culture:
Literary Criticism in Perspective

Edited by
Benjamin Franklin V
(*South Carolina*)

Editorial Board

Literary Criticism in Perspective

James Hardin (*South Carolina*), General Editor

Eitel Timm (*British Columbia*), German Literature

Benjamin Franklin V (*South Carolina*), American and English Literature

Reingard M. Nischik (*Freiburg im Breisgau*), Comparative Literature

* * *

About *Literary Criticism in Perspective*

Books in the series *Literary Criticism in Perspective*, a subseries of the series *Studies in German Literature, Linguistics, and Culture*, and *Studies in English and American Literature, Linguistics, and Culture*, trace literary scholarship and criticism on major and neglected writers alike, or on a single major work, a group of writers, a literary school or movement. In so doing the authors — authorities on the topic in question who are also well-versed in the principles and history of literary criticism — address a readership consisting of scholars, students of literature at the graduate and undergraduate level, and the general reader. One of the primary purposes of the series is to illuminate the nature of literary criticism itself, to gauge the influence of social and historic currents on aesthetic judgments once thought objective and normative.

Edward Lear and the Critics

Edward Lear: A Self-Portrait

Ann C. Colley

EDWARD LEAR AND THE CRITICS

CAMDEN HOUSE

Copyright © 1993 by
CAMDEN HOUSE, INC.

Published by Camden House, Inc.
Drawer 2025
Columbia, SC 29202 USA

Printed on acid-free paper.
Binding materials are chosen for strength and
durability.

All Rights Reserved
Printed in the United States of America
First Edition

ISBN 1-879751-80-1

Library of Congress Cataloging-in-Publication Data

Colley, Ann C.
    Edward Lear and the critics / Ann C. Colley. -- 1st ed.
      p.   cm.   -- (Studies in English and American literature,
linguistics, and culture. Literary criticism in perspective)
    Includes bibliographical references (p.) and index.
    ISBN 1-879751-80-1 (alk. paper)
    1. Lear, Edward, 1812-1888--Criticism and interpretation--History,
2. Nonsense-verses, English--History and criticism--Theory, etc.
I. Title. II. Series.
PR4879.L2Z62 1993
821'.8--dc20
                                                                               93-25216
                                                                                 CIP

Acknowledgments

IN COMPILING THE INFORMATION for this book I am greatly indebted to Majorie L. Lord, Associate Librarian and Head of Inter-Library Loan, and to Betty Plewniak, Library Assistant in the Inter-Library Loan Office, at the E. H. Butler Library at the State University College of New York at Buffalo. Both assisted me with such promptness, good humor, and interest that my work became much easier than it might otherwise have been. The task of collecting materials was also made more pleasant by Rachel Massey who spent two or three busy and full days tracking down and xeroxing articles for me from nineteenth-century periodicals at McGill University Library. I also wish to thank Wanda M. Slawinska of the E. H. Butler Library for her kindness in translating an article from Ukrainian into English and Professor Donna B. Campbell for her generous help with technical matters. As always I am indebted to Irving J. Massey, Professor of English at the State University of New York at Buffalo, whose help in translating and discussing the articles written in French, Spanish, Italian, and German made it possible for me to compose a fuller and livelier book.

For Gwen Hilary Colley

Contents

Preface   xi

1: The "Nonsenses"   1

2: Lear and Nonsense Theory   32

3: Lear the Artist and Musician   46

4: The Letters and Journals   73

5: Biographers and Collectors   84

6: Conclusion   96

Bibliography   99

Index   115

Preface

> *B was a book*
> *With a binding of blue*
> *And pictures and stories*
> *For me and for you.*
> *b!*
> *Nice little Book.*
>
> (Lear's *Nonsense Alphabet*)

WHEN MOST PEOPLE HEAR the name Edward Lear, the rhythm of his limericks, the figure of the Dong with a luminous nose, and the image of individuals hanging upside down on a plant's stalk rise to their minds. Their thoughts turn to what Lear called his "nonsenses" — to the limericks, the poems, the stories, the alphabets, and the nonsense botany — because it is they that have endured in the popular imagination. But, as those familiar with his biography know, Lear spent his life doing much more than composing his verses and stories. He earned his living as an artist; he traveled extensively and published impressions of his journeys; he occasionally set poems to music; and he wrote a large number of letters.

Because of Lear's varied talents, reviews of his work are more plentiful than, perhaps, most realize. Critics have written not only about his "nonsenses" but also about his animal and bird illustrations, his watercolors, his oil paintings, his travel journals, his correspondence, and his music. This book is a history of how critics from the nineteenth century on have regarded Lear's writing, illustrating, painting, and composing. The first chapter traces the history of critical reactions to Lear's nonsense — this, not surprisingly, is the longest chapter. The second chapter, "Lear and Nonsense Theory," discusses how critics have used Lear's verses to help them structure their idea of what nonsense is. The third chapter, "Lear: the Artist and Musician," is about how reviewers have responded to his natural history illustrations, his paintings, and his music. The fourth chapter, "The Letters and Journals," looks at the way in which critics have regarded the published letters and travel journals. And the fifth chapter, "Biographers and Collectors," surveys the biographies of Lear and glances at the books and essays written by those who have collected his manuscripts, books, drawings, and paintings.

The criticism summarized in the book is not only what was written in Great Britain and North America; it is also that which has come out of such places as Spain, Italy, Germany, France, Denmark, and the Ukraine. Because Lear's nonsense has been translated into a number of languages, it is to be expected that literary scholars from other parts of the world should have taken an interest in it. And because Lear traveled to places like Greece and India, it is not surprising that scholars in these countries have wanted to comment upon his paintings and journals. Within each of these chapters, I have attempted to include as many of the critics as possible. As a result, each chapter is comprehensive, but not exhaustive. Given Lear's extensive and international reputation, it would be an almost impossible task either to identify or even mention every piece of commentary.

In writing the book I have kept five goals in mind. One is to give a chronological sense of the various responses to Lear's writing, painting, and composing. The second is to offer an overview of these critical reactions by identifying patterns of thought that run through them. The third is to allow those who wish to contribute to Lear scholarship a chance to read about what other critics have said so that they might work within or react to that context. The fourth is to expand people's knowledge of Lear's work by offering background information about his life and by helping readers understand the breadth of his talents and accomplishments. The final goal is to bring under one cover a community of scholars who are often segregated from one another. Because of language differences and because of the nature of academia that does not always allow for an easy interaction of ideas — in spite of recent technological advances, and, perhaps, even because of a certain degree of nationalism or sense of ownership on the part of a few critics — some miss the opportunity of an equal hearing or the chance to exchange or acknowledge each other's ideas. I hope this survey of criticism helps alter these realities and provides a kind of meeting ground.

What this book does not do, however, is properly represent Lear. To talk about Lear without displaying his wry, ironic, and self-deprecating nonsense drawings or his watercolor sketches and natural history prints is unfair because for Lear words and images are always inseparable. It is difficult to separate them here and to offer a book that does not have both "pictures and stories / For me and for you." Still I hope it is a "Nice little book" — at least, a helpful one. As one of the Camden House series entitled "Literary Criticism in Perspective," the book traces the criticism of Lear's work so that scholars, students of literature at the graduate and undergraduate levels, and the general reader may have a better sense of how people in the nineteenth and twentieth centuries have responded to his work and what some of their major preoccupations have been.

1: The "Nonsenses"

> There was an Old Derry down Derry,
> Who loved to see little folks merry;
> So he made them a book, and with laughter they shook
> At the fun of that Derry down Derry
>
> (from the title page of *A Book of Nonsense*)

EVER SINCE THE FIRST *A Book of Nonsense* appeared in 1846, few readers have found it possible to turn its pages and remain silent. Such is the infectious charm of the jingling rhymes and such is the mysterious appeal of the verses' incongruities that readers and critics have wanted to register their reactions. They have, as it were, felt compelled to offer a commentary upon a genre that can be simultaneously frivolous and profound, concrete and elusive.

Upon the publication of subsequent editions of Lear's nonsense and with the passing of time, these critical responses have accumulated to form a considerable body of criticism. And now that Lear finally has his place among the eminent Victorians, the criticism flourishes. Lear's "nonsenses," as he called them, are no longer a subject only for British and American critics; they are also a subject for scholars from, for instance, the Ukraine, Italy, Germany, and Greece. Lear's reputation has traveled farther than even Lear himself did. It has gone "out in the world beyond" to the "Gromboolian plain" of criticism and on into the "Torrible zone" of analysis. Although Lear was aware that people enjoyed his verses, he never aspired to have the nonsense carry him out of his century into ours. One can almost imagine the mixture of pleasure and annoyance if he were to know how many reviewers and critics have settled on his work, like the birds who nest in the Old Man's beard or perch on his nose, and have found him an intriguing resting place.

Sometimes the criticism reflects a particular moment in time, but, perhaps more frequently, it seems to keep turning back upon itself. That is to say, the criticism often appears to be a series of variations upon a number of recurring themes. For instance, throughout the years critics have remarked upon Lear's verbal playfulness — for example, his borascible, propitious, capricious, and ombliferous adjectives — and a few have lingered over his linguistic structures. Some have regarded the verses as pieces of "harmless gaiety" written out of innocent fun; others, however, have wondered if there is not a satirical motive or, at least, a commentary on an oppressive social code. A few critics have thought the nonsenses incapable of possessing any symbolic meaning; many more, though, have regarded them as vehicles for Lear to express his loneliness and address his difficulties or, perhaps, to mask the workings of his subconscious. A number of critics have applauded the nonsense verses for their joyous rebellion against sense — for representing a world in which people like the Young Lady of Norway get flattened by doors and unperturbed remark, "What of that?" or a place where a "Queer Querulous Quail" smokes a pipe on top of a Tin Tea-Kettle — others, though, have admired them for their sense. Some critics have recognized Lear's indebtedness to Romanticism; others have spoken of the verses' and stories' affinity to surrealism; yet others have traced the history of the limerick's form. Not surprisingly a number have also remarked on the nonsense drawings — how difficult it would be to resist the figures whose arms spread out in cheerful acceptance of adversity or pull rigidly behind them keeping the old man or the young woman suspended between contentment and anger, standing and sitting — and still more have not been able to resist the temptation to compare Lear's work with Lewis Carroll's.

Throughout the chronological narrative that follows, these themes and preoccupations come in and out of focus. If a theme disappears for a while it is not lost, but merely out of view. Like the cow belonging to the "invidious Old Man of Aösta," the idea has simply climbed a tree — it is momentarily out of sight; it will come down again, but, perhaps, slightly altered by its experience away. Not all the criticism is repetitive; however, for there are moments of originality that allow the reader to see Lear's nonsense from a fresh perspective.

Nineteenth-Century Criticism

Although the first and second editions of *A Book of Nonsense* (1846 and 1856) seem to have elicited few reviews, they did not go unnoticed. Rumors circulated, for instance, concerning the identity of "old Derry down Derry." (It was not until the 1861 edition that Lear used his own name.) Many speculated that since the verses were dedicated to the children of Knowsley Hall, the Early of Derby was the author, and yet others thought that no such person as Edward Lear lived, a misconception Lear apparently came face to face with when he met a gentleman who told him so. Fortunately Lear had his name inside his hat and was able to correct and silence the disbeliever.

Lear's limericks were almost immediately popular among his contemporaries. Such was the hold on people's imagination that in 1889 a reviewer for the October 5 issue of *The Saturday Review* exclaimed, "If there flourishes in the United Kingdom a man or woman of a greater age than four years who has no knowledge whatever of the *Book of Nonsense*, that individual is much to be pitied" (388). And within a few years the limericks traveled far and wide so that in 1888 when Sir Edmund Strachey reviewed the nonsense verses for *The Quarterly Review,* he was able to refer to English owners of a cattle ranch in New Mexico who used as their trade-mark Lear's drawing of the "old man, who said, how shall I flee from this terrible cow?" (358). Furthermore these limericks accompanied the British when they went out to the colonial protectorates so that when Lear traveled to places like Corfu or India, he was often lionized by adults and children who were familiar with his nonsense poems and stories. Moreover many motivated by the charm of Lear's verses attempted to imitate them. There was, in fact, a "limerick craze." Indeed Lear's nonsense verses attracted enough imitators that a reviewer for the December 25, 1871, issue of *The Times* felt obligated to warn his readers that "Nothing is more difficult" than to write nonsense. And five years later a reviewer for *The Examiner* (November 18, 1876) deemed it necessary to complain that since the appearance of the 1871 volume of nonsense a "great many attempts have been made to imitate what seems to be so easy" (1302) and have failed — a truism that, perhaps, our own attempts have proved to be all too correct.

One indication of the limericks' popularity is that reviewers chose to enter the nonsense books into the Christmas list sections of magazines. These lists are among the earliest of the "official" notices of Lear's nonsense writing. Among these, for instance, is one that appears in the December 21, 1861, issue of *The Saturday Review*. Here the reviewer places Lear's *A Book of Nonsense* next to such other titles as Keats's *Poetical Works*, Carolyn Norton's *The Lady of La Garaye*, and books of riddles and double acrostics (646) — a placement that for those who find both witty and romantic or poetic elements in Lear's nonsense is not as inappropriate or absurd as it might seem.

When the reviewers are not merely listing Lear's nonsense, they are dwelling upon its comic delights or its "innocent mirth." A writer in the January 18, 1871, *Judy, or the London Serio-Comic Journal* speaks jocularly of *A Book of Nonsense* as providing a "good laugh" for all ages (114); the reviewer for the December 24, 1870, issue of *The Saturday Review* calls *Nonsense Songs* "a very comical little book" (814), and Sidney Colvin writing in the January 15, 1872, issue of *The Academy* refers to *More Nonsense* as a "stout jovial book" that "transcends any kind of criticism" (23–24). These expressions of delight continue so that in 1876 the reviewer for *The Saturday*

Review admires Lear for the "masterly ease with which he introduces foreign yet melodious words, full of music" (734), and the one for the September 17, 1887, issue of *The Spectator* praises "The Story of the Four Little Children Who Went Round the World" as a "most exquisite piece of imaginative absurdity" (1251–52).

Among the most interesting of these early enthusiastic responses to the nonsense is the one in the December 17, 1870, issue of *The Spectator*. Here the reviewer speaks not only of Lear's verses but also of the nature of nonsense itself. He refers to Lear's earlier nonsense writing as being a "gay rebellion against sense" but always within the boundaries of sense. According to this writer's judgment, true nonsense should "never go far enough from sense to lose the feeling of the delightful freedom which is implied in rebellion" (1506) — an interesting idea that theorists who believe that nonsense emerges from the tension between meaning and non-meaning quite rightly develop. Perhaps the most-often repeated of these positive responses to Lear's nonsense is John Ruskin's. In a brief article he wrote for *The Pall Mall Magazine* (February 15, 1886), Ruskin speaks of *A Book of Nonsense* as "surely the most beneficent and innocent of all books yet produced" for the public. He finds the verses "inimitable and refreshing and perfect in rhythm." He concludes, "I really don't know any other author to whom I am half so grateful, for my idle self, as Edward Lear. I shall put him first of my hundred authors." Ruskin's is, perhaps, a qualified enthusiasm, for how good is idleness from such an industrious person's perspective? All the same, though, Lear was deeply satisfied and complimented to be recognized by this eminent critic. Lear immediately sent Ruskin a copy of "Incidents in the Life of my Uncle Arly," his last and poignantly autobiographical piece of nonsense.

Not all of Lear's contemporaries, it should be pointed out, were as consistently enchanted as the majority. Frequently the criticism registered disappointment that Lear's later or more recent work did not measure up to the earliest. The critic for the December 17, 1870, issue of *The Spectator*, for example, thinks there are moments in *Nonsense Songs, Stories, Botany, and Alphabets* that are so "far-fetched" that the "sense of effort destroys" the true character of nonsense (1506). A reviewer, perhaps the same one, writing for a later (December 23, 1871) issue of the magazine suggests that the rhymes of the new nonsense are not as good as the earlier and that Lear relies too much upon exaggeration and verbal play. The publication of *Laughable Lyrics* elicited similar responses. A reviewer for the December 2, 1876, issue of *The Spectator* remarks on how the most recent volume demonstrates the difficulties of continuing to write good nonsense. And the critic for *The Athenaeum* (November 18, 1876) finds "The Nonsense Botany" rather "trite" and "mannered" (664). He finds the exaggerated gestures disconcerting. Previous successes can stultify. The anxiety of one's own influence is, perhaps, even more threatening than that emanating from a predecessor.

Some of Lear's contemporaries even found fault with the drawings because of their childish distortions. Angus Davidson, for instance, tells the story of a Madame de Bunsen who would not allow her children and grandchildren to glance at them "for fear the precious infants' 'sense of the beautiful' might be damaged" (187).

These more negative critiques, though, did little to dampen the majority's enthusiasm. One reason the nonsense was appealing to so many critics is that it expressed a "harmless gaiety" and innocence (a word chosen by Ruskin). It was not "vulgar." A reviewer in the September 17, 1887, issue of *The Spectator* distinguishes Lear from all his followers by stating that his nonsense is "void of vulgarity" (1251). Another reviewer writing for *The Examiner* remarks not only upon the "irrepressible humour" but also upon the "healthy satire" (826) within the nonsense verses (December 24, 1870).

The reference to "satire" in the previous reviewer's remarks is, of course, part of another issue — the question of intentionality — that concerned the contemporary critics. A significant number of the nineteenth-century critics believe that Lear's nonsense has no ulterior motive. The nonsense is as Lear proclaimed it to be in his preface to the third edition of *A Book of Nonsense* — it is "pure and absolute" nonsense. According to these critics, there is no specific political or personal satire intended. The nonsense is only a "joyous rebellion against sense" or "a free gallop into the impossible" (*The Spectator*, December 23, 1871, 1570). Two later reviewers in *The Spectator* echo this opinion. One proclaims the nonsense verses and stories "incapable of being made to harbor any symbolical meaning" (September 17, 1887, 1251), and the other observes that "if Mr. Lear twists words into fanciful and grotesque forms, it is with no malice prepense, with no ulterior motive" (April 9, 1887, 492).

Other critics, however, were willing to admit that there was a general, but "gentle" satire in the nonsense. In a March 24, 1888, issue of *The Saturday Review*, one critic speaks of the nonsense as "a mild species of genuine satire" (361). And another in *The Athenaeum* (January 13, 1872) speaks of Lear's nonsense botany as "a good-humoured satire on the practice of the learned, or rather tasteless botanists, in bestowing on plants names as hideous as they are inept" (43). This critic also finds an "undercurrent of thought and satire on 'things in general'" in the limericks (43).

The publication of the nonsense books sometimes caused members of the public to wonder if the verses had a political meaning and if the drawings caricatured known individuals. In particular, "There was an old man at a Station" (*More Nonsense*) caught people's attention, for it seems to criticize the unpopular Gladstone and his habit of making speeches at railway stations.

For instance, the reviewer for the September 17, 1887, issue of *The Spectator* concludes his article entitled "Lear's Nonsense Books" with a set of amusing and challenging examination questions on the verses and songs. The writer, apparently determined to expose what he considered to be the limerick's political satire, could not resist pointing out the limerick's opening two lines ("There was an old man at a Station / Who made a promiscuous oration") and wryly inquiring: "What bearing may we assume the foregoing couplet to have upon Mr. Lear's political views?" (1252).

The understanding that Lear's nonsense belongs to a long literary tradition is another topic of discussion for the contemporary reviewers. His nonsense is not extraneous to what one might now call the literary canon. The first major article on this matter is Sir Edmund Strachey's long review of the twenty-sixth edition of *A Book of Nonsense; Nonsense Songs, Stories, Botany, and Alphabets; More Nonsense, Pictures, Rhymes, Botany, Laughable Lyrics, a Fourth Book of Nonsense, Poems, Songs, Botany, Music.* Strachey's article, entitled "Nonsense as a Fine Art," places Lear in a literary tradition that includes Chaucer, Shakespeare, Milton, Wordsworth, and Tennyson. Lear's work is not something unworthy to be placed with that of these poets. Strachey, however, is not the first to make such connections. For instance, a critic writing for the December 9, 1876, issue of *The Saturday Review* compares Lear's lyrical and musical qualities to those of Milton, Scott, and Aeschylus. This critic suggests that "The Cummerbund" (a late nonsense poem) "may rank, in its way, with Shelley's 'Lines to an Indian Air'" (734). And another reviewer in the September 17, 1887, issue of *The Spectator* speaks of "The Dong with the Luminous Nose" as being "a sort-of nonsense version of the love of Nausicaa for Ulysses, only that the sexes are inverted." In his mind Lear is "a genuine and graceful artist" who writes "melodious" verses (1251) — an observation that twentieth-century critics have developed, especially as they have emphasized Lear's indebtedness to Romanticism in the composition of his nonsense songs.

As we have seen, through the example of Madame de Bunsen, the nineteenth-century critics were also interested in the drawings that Lear created to accompany the nonsense verses and stories. Although some thought them childlike, many thought them superior to the verses and discovered an artistic and mature hand behind them. The reviewer for *The Spectator* (September 17, 1887) writes, for instance, that "Generally speaking, these designs are, as it were, an idealisation of the efforts of a clever child ..." (1251). But a year later in *The Saturday Review* (March 24, 1888), a critic refutes this point of view when he observes, "the drawings very cunningly combine the clumsy conventions dear to children with types and expressions that display real artistic knowledge and observation ..." (361) — an opinion Strachey shares, for in his "Nonsense as a Fine Art" he exclaims, "None but a humourist could have poured out such a flood of laughable absurdities, and only an artist could have given with such a free hand all the grotesque forms in which he pretends to emulate the awkward scrawls of the school-boy on his slate" (359).

Other interesting points that the critics identify are that Lear makes nonsense believable (*The Pall Mall Magazine,* November 25, 1871) and that many of his subjects are eccentrics who receive harsh treatment from others (*The Spectator,* September 17, 1887) or "gallantly bear their eccentricities and nobly disregard any of those inconveniences which ensue upon the indulgence of personal eccentricity" (*The Saturday Review,* March 24, 1888, 361–62).

These various critical perspectives do not fade away with the closing of the nineteenth century. They pass through the artificial border of time and cross over into the twentieth century for other critics to take them up and shape them according to their particular concerns and tastes. The lure of the limericks, the melancholy absurdity of Lear's songs, the adventurous, yet oddly comfortable, voyages to exotic places, and the swift and liberating lines of his illustrations continue to fascinate readers and invite them to linger over and comment upon them. In a way, the "nonsenses," while taking people out of themselves, by offering them a means of escape, also often invite them to address the difficulties they, like Lear, wish to leave behind.

Twentieth-Century Responses:
The Early Years

In the first few decades after the turn of the century, a handful of Lear's friends and those who remembered reading his nonsense in their own childhood began to write about Lear and, thereby, contributed to the continuing appeal of his nonsense writing. Such was the popularity of the nonsenses that when Walter Jerrold reviewed Lady Strachey's 1911 *Queery Leary Nonsense: A Lear Nonsense Book*, he claimed to be both horrified and surprised that some of his acquaintances were not familiar with them. In an article for *The Bookman*, he exclaims that one of his friends "is old enough to have been brought up on fairly early editions" of the nonsense books, but "she knew not Lear!" (148).

This 1911 edition of the nonsense verses is an important one, for not only does it reflect the public's continuing desire to read the verses but also shows how Lear's friends became involved in making the work available and keeping the memory of him "green." Lady Strachey, for instance, was the niece of Lear's close friends Lady Waldegrave and Lord Carlingford. The occasion for the new edition was additional, unpublished material (drawings and verses) that friends like the Earl of Northbrook and Hubert Congreve had made available. Because of Lord Cromer's particular generosity, Lady Strachey asked him to write an introduction. In his opening remarks Lord Cromer seems primarily interested in reporting his own remembrances. For him Lear's nonsense "constituted one of the delights and solaces of his life" (11). He recalls that Lear "perhaps occasionally felt some slight disappointment that his fame rested not so much on his merits as an artist" (11) as it did on his reputation as a nonsense writer — an opinion that the reviewer, Jerrold, does not share. He believes quite the opposite is true and records Thomas Congreve's words: "I have always believed that in his heart of hearts he was prouder of his 'Book of Nonsense' than of his paintings" (*The Bookman*, 149). It is interesting to note that both Lord Cromer and Jerrold introduce a biographical note into their criticism, and, in this way, set a precedent for those critics who later explore more rigorously the relationship between Lear's nonsense and his life. Their point of view is notably different from G. K. Chesterton's who in his 1908 article on Lear for *The Nation* decides to turn his back on the "real" Lear so that he can enjoy the nonsensical one (123). Chesterton found Lear's life to be too painful; it intruded upon the humor.

In addition to the question of the biographical elements in the nonsense writing, all these reviewers in the early decades of the twentieth century continue to be interested in naming the qualities that distinguish Lear's nonsense from others'. One of the most important publications in this respect is Emile Cammaerts's *The Poetry of Nonsense* (1925). In this study Cammaerts, concerned that the genre has not received enough serious attention, identifies and describes the idiosyncracies of nonsense. Lear's writing, of course, is an important topic in his discussion. Many of the qualities of Lear's work that Cammaerts identifies are familiar in the sense that they reflect characteristics already noticed in the earlier more modest reviews. To begin with Cammaerts insists that Lear's nonsense has no political motive. It asks to be enjoyed for its own sake. In stressing that it seems entirely free from satire and parody, Cammaerts is echoing, among others, Lord Cromer's belief that Lear was "too warm-hearted to be satirical" (11), and he is following Jerrold's suggestion that Lear's nonsense is just nonsense and nothing else but nonsense. Cammaerts stresses that it is not "a mask for the disguising of the ironic and the sardonic" (149). Significantly all of these critics, especially Cromer and Cammaerts, tend to agree that Lear directs the humor against himself rather than toward others. And how active that tendency of Lear's was. One need only to look at the many self-portraits Lear did to see how he, through these cartoons, exaggerated what bothered him most (e.g. his nose and, later, his stoutness) and how he also drew himself in awkward positions — at the mercy of a recalcitrant horse or a mocking Foss (Lear's cat) — to create laughter and cause the viewer to smile rather than to sympathize with him.

We have seen that in the nineteenth century a number of reviewers had remarked upon the romantic elements within Lear's nonsense (for instance, the December 9, 1876, article in *The Saturday Review;* the September 17, 1871, review in *The Spectator,* and Strachey's "Nonsense as a Fine Art" in *The Quarterly Review*). Cammaerts picks up this theme again in order to emphasize the emotional and poetical elements within Lear's poetry — his nonsense songs. He is especially taken with its musical qualities. He suggests that Lear, as well as Lewis Carroll, can be associated with Ruskin and Tennyson, for there is "a certain connection between the attitude of mind of the old and modern Romanticists and that of Nonsense writers. They make the same appeal to the imagination; they rely on ... sentiment more than intellect" (85). Other early twentieth-century critics also notice this correspondence. For instance, Chesterton writing over ten years before Cammaerts likes to think of Lear's nonsense as being "emotional and poetical," and remarks upon its long rolling romantic lines (124). Later in 1933 T. S. Eliot lectured at Scripps College on "Edward Lear and Modern Poetry." (According to William Baker's 1983 article on the subject, the lecture is now lost.) During that lecture he remarked upon a number of similarities between Lear and such poets as Tennyson, Swinburne, and Mallarmé. The comparison between Lear and these poets recurs so that, for instance, critics in the 1960s and 1970s continue to remark upon it.

Like his predecessors Cammaerts also pays considerable attention to Lear's nonsense drawings. He too admires them and finds within them an artistic hand. As if defending Lear against those who have thought his drawings merely childish, Cammaerts speaks of their being "at once childish, deliberately exaggerated and irresistibly funny." He adds, "No artist or connoisseur will question the intentional character of these 'mistakes'" (67). Cammaerts is especially sensitive to Lear's ability to create a harmony between the illustration and the text, between the matter and the form.

Cammaerts's study allowed people to think more carefully about Lear's nonsense. For instance, Muriel Kent in "The Art of Nonsense," written for *The Cornhill Magazine* (1934), was able to use Cammaerts's discussion and add it to what she learned from Walter de la Mare's study of Lewis Carroll so that she might be able to understand better Lear's inventive genius. In her article Kent recalls how delighted de la Mare is to discover Lear — "this hybrid flourishing in the cultivated garden" (478) — for he comes quite unexpectedly, in her words, into a world that had usually been "nourished on stories, hymns, and poems that contained fearful warnings blended with moral instruction" (478). Both he and Carroll escaped from that "stiff and frigid world ... into that kingdom which remains unexplored by the generality and undesired save by its freeborn sons" (479).

In this article Kent also touches upon the various characteristics of Lear's nonsense, the question of the limerick's origin (she recounts the story that the word "may have been partly due to the somewhat earlier Learic, coined ... from Edward Lear" [480]), the argument over Lear's refusal to use "a strong last line" (480), his mixing the credible with the unusual, and the role of the "they" (de la Mare calls this choric voice "perhaps the greatest triumph" of Lear's inventions [481]). Quoting extensively from Cammaerts, she also refers to the Englishness of nonsense and to Lear's exquisite sense of rhythm and poetry.

Throughout these early decades, the phrase "the master of nonsense" belongs to Lear. Frequently reviewers compare his work to Carroll's and find Lear's nonsense to be superior. Chesterton writes, for instance, "Edward Lear was greater than Lewis Carroll; at least, he could do what Lewis Carroll could not do. Lewis Carroll's nonsense was merely mathematical and logical. Edward Lear's was emotional and poetical" (123–24). Cammaerts too seems to regard Lear's nonsense as being superior, for not only is it poetic but also highly original. In his opinion Lear "goes further than other writers," for he "creates a brand-new nonsense world of his own ..." (47). It is interesting to note, by the way, that Lear and Carroll never met each other, nor did they comment upon each other's work.

Critics in the 1930s continue to refer to Lear as "the master of nonsense." For instance, F. J. Darton in *Children's Books in England: Five Centuries of Social Life* (1932) considers Lear's nonsense books to be better than other humorous children's books published in the early part of Victoria's reign. He believes they display an "eminence" that the others lack (256). It is, perhaps, not surprising then to find that the title of R. L. Mégroz's lengthy article on Lear for *The Cornhill Magazine* (1938) is "The Master of Nonsense." In this article Mégroz worries that the public only has a vague sense of who Lear is and, worse, has forgotten the variety of his nonsense. They tend to think only of *A Book of Nonsense* and the nonsense songs; they forget the nonsense alphabets, stories, botany, and cookery. Mégroz wants to persuade his readers to take Lear's work more seriously and to pay more attention to all of it. He instructs his audience that Lear really created a new genre of nonsense. His is not the older satirical form. (Previously, according to Mégroz, nonsense had been primarily a satirical mode of expression.) Lear's is a purer nonsense, freer of politics and references to particular people. His is a more universal absurdity.

Mégroz also lauds the nonsense illustrations, and as if the praises of their merits uttered by the critics decades before had fallen on unwilling ears, he reiterates the defense of Lear's artistic talent. He refuses to join those who think of the drawings as being simply childish.

Generally speaking, the human figures are sheer nonsense, true enough to something in the artist himself, yet marvelously child-like in manner (though much better drawn than anything done by a child); while the non-human forms constantly reveal a highly sophisticated technique subdued to the nonsensical *élan*. (178).

To help convince his readers of Lear's importance Mégroz also discusses the influence Lear had on other illustrators and nonsense writers by naming those in England, on the continent, and in America who are, he says, indebted to Lear. The list includes such illustrators as Doré, Caran D'Ache, and Wilhelm Busch, and such limerick writers as D. G. Rossetti, Swinburne, and even Tennyson.

Like others before him, Mégroz cannot resist the temptation of comparing Lear and Carroll. For him Lear is the better nonsense writer because Carroll's verse, "though clever, misses Lear's spontaneity in effect and usually makes wit supply the lack of fantasy. And while his [Carroll's] artfully made portmanteau words are excellent to convey suggestion, they are not created like Lear's coined words for atmosphere and music" (189).

As important as Cammaerts's and Mégroz's contributions are, they are not as substantial as Angus Davidson's 1938 biography, *Edward Lear: Landscape Painter and Nonsense Poetry*. In this first full-length study of Lear's life and work, Davidson discusses Lear's nonsense writing, but it is a segment that takes second place to a consideration of Lear's artistic career. Consequently, even though Davidson admires the limericks and poems and finds Lear's genius in them, he devotes proportionally fewer pages to them than most critics had up to this point. Not surprisingly Davidson recognizes the originality of the nonsense drawings and admires Lear's mastery of the line. He remarks upon how Lear's hand controls the pen and makes it "do things which are surprising, whimsical, but always deliberate" (188). As wonderful and exhilarating as these drawings are, it is, Davidson believes, the nonsense poems that should "take first place." He praises them for two main reasons: they are a new invention — nothing like them had been written before — and they express deeper feelings than the other nonsense verses. The later and longer poems, like "The Dong with a Luminous Nose," "The Pelican Chorus," "The Courtship of the Yonghy-Bonghy-Bò," "The Owl and the Pussycat," "The Duck and the Kangaroo," "The Jumblies," and "The Table and the Chair," especially, express a loneliness, a feeling of isolation. They reveal Lear's sense of himself as a "spectator" and, perhaps, a failure. Like a number of critics before him Davidson also admires these poems for their rhythmical and poetic sense, especially for their sensitivity to sound. The result is that when Davidson submits to the temptation to compare Lear and Carroll, he concludes that Lear is "greater" because he is the "greater poet" (198).

Although, perhaps, Davidson in his discussion concerning the nonsense writing often reflects what other critics have already observed, he does, through the biographical details, lend a legitimacy to reading a life into the nonsense verses and, therefore, makes it easier for later critics to place Lear's nonsense confidently within the biographical context. (One early instance of this is the article by S. A. Nock in the 1941 *Sewanee Review* entitled "Lacrimae Nugarum: Edward Lear of the Nonsense Verses." He reads the nonsense verses as Lear's "emotional biography.") Furthermore, Davidson emphasizes one characteristic of the nonsense that subsequent readers have also found important. This characteristic is the use of the "they" in the limericks. (An example would be "There was an Old Man with a gong, / Who bumped it all day long; / But they called out, 'O law! you're a horrid old bore!' / So they smashed that Old Man with a gong.") Through examples, Davidson explains that the "they" is the force of public opinion that interferes with the individual's sense of freedom. The "they" is an "inquisitive, conventional, and almost always uncharitable" group (196). It should be noted that Aldous Huxley, in his 1920 essay on Lear for *The Athenaeum* (later reprinted in *On the Margin*, 1933), had already remarked on the "they" of the nonsense rhymes and had identified them as "Right-Thinking Men and Women" who represent public opinion (*On the Margin,* 169). In his article, Huxley speaks of how offensive and dull the "they" can be.

The 1940s and 1950s
The identity of the "they" in the limericks continues to fascinate critics in the 1940s and 1950s. For instance, the subject catches George Orwell's attention. In an essay which eventually appeared in *Shooting an Elephant and Other Essays* (1950), Orwell, referring to Huxley, agrees that the "they" are the realists (those who are anti-art), "the practical men, the sober citizens in bowler hats who are always anxious to stop you doing anything worth doing" (182). Most of this article, though, is a response to R. L. Mégroz's 1945 edition of Lear's verses and poems entitled *The Lear Omnibus*. (There were a number of new editions of Lear's nonsense in the 1940s.) Although Orwell reiterates or paraphrases much of what Mégroz says about Lear, he also qualifies Mégroz's enthusiasm and, in so doing, reveals his impatience with some of Lear's nonsense. Orwell finds Lear "silly and tiresome" when he is too "arbitrary" and "gives his fancy free play." For instance, Orwell does not care for "Three Receipts for Domestic Cooking." As if echoing the nineteenth-century critics who were impatient with the later nonsense because it seemed forced and as if agreeing with those who enjoyed the nonsense because it never completely left the boundaries of sense, Orwell prefers Lear's nonsense when it is plausible, when "a touch of burlesque or perverted logic

makes its appearance." As an example he cites two lines from "The Pobble Who Has no Toes":

It's a fact the whole world knows
That Pobbles are happier without toes.

These lines are uttered by the aunt after the Pobble returns with his toes eaten off by some unidentified creature. They carry an element of sense or a hint of logic that makes the words funny. Orwell's explanation is interesting to read, for it reveals his own political bias. He suggests that the aunt's remark is humorous "because it has a meaning, and one might even say a political significance. For the whole theory of authoritarian government is summed up in the statement that Pobbles were happier without their toes" (183).

Contrary to most enthusiasts, Orwell finds Carroll funnier than Lear, for Carroll is less fantastic. (Orwell believed that one should not set out deliberately to write nonsense.) Furthermore, Orwell disagrees with Mégroz on the point of Lear's beneficial influence on literature. Arguing with Mégroz's claim, Orwell writes that Lear is "not altogether a good influence," for his nonsense writing is responsible for the "silly whimsiness of present-day children's books" (184). Orwell does concede, however, that Lear's effect on "comic draughtmanship" is beneficial. At the conclusion of his essay, Orwell makes an interesting point that no critic has subsequently developed. He suggests that nonsense "is best produced gradually and accidentally by communities rather than by individuals" (184). As far as I know not even the nonsense theorists have explored this suggestive perspective.

Of all the critical work done on Lear in the 1950s, Elizabeth Sewell's important study of nonsense, *The Field of Nonsense* (1952), is, perhaps, the most significant, for it influenced so many other critics. In her book Sewell concentrates upon the writings of Lear and Carroll, for they are, in her words, the "masters of their craft" (4). When Sewell refers to them, it becomes readily apparent that unlike many other critics who are eager either to explore the link between these authors' writing and their lives or to uncover their "sub-conscious" text (6), she wants only to reveal the structure of their nonsense. She is neither interested in psychoanalysis nor in the biographical details. It is, rather, within a formal context that she prefers to discuss Lear's work. Sewell sees as her primary task the isolating of the characteristics that create nonsense. When she turns her attention to Lear's verses, she identifies a number of qualities. Lear's nonsense is a world of things, words, and language; it is a world that delights in number and shows interest "in meticulous and well-ordered detail" (44); it is an orderly world that is run like a game with rules and delights in serialization of everyday things. Here the only emotion is the feeling of isolation "since it emphasizes the unattached nature of the player" (145) within the framework of the game of nonsense. If any other emotion enters, then the nonsense dwindles. With this principle in mind, Sewell judges Lear's longer poems to be "failures," for they admit too much and reveal a Lear who is neither detached nor in control. The sense of "security, freedom, and purely mental delight" that constitutes his true nonsense disappears under the stress of "a sense of reality and earnestness" (149). (For a more complete discussion of Sewell see chapter 2.)

In spite of Sewell's insistence that nonsense fails if it admits too much feeling, critics of the 1950s persisted in admiring Lear's verses for their emotional quality and refused to acknowledge that such feelings detracted from their absurdity. For instance, J. T. Brockway in "Edward Lear, Poet" (1950) recognizes a "mixture of tragedy, gentleness, and innocence" in the "nonsenses." He argues that it is these qualities that make the verses so appealing. Similarly, C. M. Bowra in *The Romantic Imagination* (1950) delights in the verses' melancholy. Both Brockway and Bowra revive Chesterton's and Cammaerts's belief that Lear's nonsense approaches the poetry of the Romantic poets. In particular, they consider the musical, rhythmical, and lyrical elements in the longer poems. Like Poe's verses, these poems express a sense of failure and misery. They possess "a melting sweetness." Their "images of grief are wedded to a haunting melody" (Bowra, 278).

The connection between Lear's nonsense and his life which critics in the early part of the century had partially explored and which, of course, Davidson and Nock had more fully considered once more comes to the surface in Jørgen Andersen's 1950 article, "Edward Lear and the Origin of Nonsense." Andersen, a Dutch critic, opens his article by offering the reader a brief sketch of Lear's life — one that is riddled with errors, partially because he is relying on Davidson's biography to tell the story of Lear's childhood and partially because in summarizing an intricate life, he falls into the trap of selecting those details which distort rather than explicate its ups and downs. Andersen suggests how Lear used nonsense as a means of "self-defence" in difficult moments. When he was angry, Andersen points out, Lear twisted his bitterness into nonsense, and, in this way, saved himself from despair. At other times he translated or transformed his nervousness and his fears into his humorous drawings. Andersen observes:

> In Lear's limerick drawings, grasshoppers, the size of human beings, creep on the backs of people, and one man has the empty eyes of a fish and a frill like fins down his shirt front. It is less fierce, but in spirit not unlike Blake's terrifying insect-men. (164)

New editions in the 1950s reflect Lear's continuing popular appeal. One example is Holbrook Jackson's *The Complete Nonsense of Edward Lear* (1951

— the collection originally appeared in 1947). This edition brings together and once more introduces the four volumes of nonsense published in Lear's lifetime (the original editions of *A Book of Nonsense; Nonsense Songs, Stories, Botany and Alphabets; More Nonsense,* and *Laughable Lyrics*). In the introduction, "Edward Lear: Laureate of Nonsense," Jackson suggests that the limericks are the safety-valve of Lear's consciousness, for they lead him away from his difficulties with his ill health and troubled finances. Furthermore they protect him, temporarily, from his "over-strung sensibility" (x). They and their drawings also reveal Lear's childishness — his "invincible boyishness" (xiii). Something in Lear would not, Jackson believes, grow up.

Lear's "game of monkeying with words" (xxiv) — his puns, Wellerisms, phonetic spelling, spoonerisms, and portmanteau words — delights Jackson. All these quick-witted tricks, though, cannot keep up with Lear's thoughts. Jackson remarks on Lear's sense that his thoughts are "ever in advance" of his words, and makes the interesting and original suggestion that Lear composed his limericks in "an instinctive effort to bridge a gap between idea and expression." Consequently, his nonsense verses are "ahead rather than behind his senses" (xxiv). This suggestive observation could quite fruitfully, I believe, be applied when one thinks about the relationship of Lear's words and images, and considers how his drawings always seem to register his thoughts and jump out faster than his words.

The 1960s and 1970s

One of the last points Jackson makes in his introduction to *The Complete Nonsense of Edward Lear* is that there are few examples left of the earliest editions of the nonsense, for they have been "used up, or eaten up, by the children for whom they were written" (xxviii).

By 1964 the British Museum had acquired the missing volumes and had, therefore, made the earliest editions more accessible to scholars. The Museum's collection of Lear editions is the subject of an article by Howard M. Nixon for the *British Museum Quarterly*. Nixon opens his article by confirming what Jackson has had to say about the earliest editions. Nixon writes:

> All early editions of Edward Lear's *A Book of Nonsense* are rare and the surviving examples are usually imperfect, having been read to pieces. Nothing before the tenth edition of 1863 was sent to the copyright libraries and it was not until after the Second World War that the Museum started to acquire earlier examples. (7)

What follows is an informative short essay on the publishing of *A Book of Nonsense*. Nixon points out, for instance, that the first edition, published by Thos. McLean in 1846, came out in two parts (price 3/6 each), and that it was not until 1861 that the nonsense books were taken over by Routledge, Warne & Routledge (who specialized in children's books) and *A Book of Nonsense* became a best seller.

In the 1960s it becomes increasingly clear that Lear's international reputation is spreading. For instance, there are translations of his verses into French and German. One example is Henri Parisot's translations of the limericks into French (*Edward Lear: limericks et autres poèmes ineptes,* 1968), another is a German translation of thirty-five limericks by H. C. Artmann, a poet of some note in modern Germany (*Edward Lears Nonsense-Verse,* 1964), and yet another is Grete Fischer's translation, *Wie nett, Herrn Lear zu Kennen. Reime und Geschichten von Edward Lear ins Deutsche Übertragen,* 1965. Furthermore scholarly articles begin appearing in foreign journals. One example is Cristóbal Serra's "Dos principes del absurdismo inglés: Edward Lear - Lewis Carroll" in *Papeles de Son Armandans* (1965). In this article Serra identifies Lear with the surrealists, but he qualifies that identification. From his point of view, Lear is deliberately absurd. He consciously selects his materials, whereas the surrealists attempt to tap the unconscious images and the unchosen words.

A number of biographies appeared in the 1960s. First Joanna Richardson's monograph on Lear appeared as part of a series for the British Council. In this monograph, Richardson devotes one section to Lear "The Nonsense Poet." Like Jackson and others before him, she too suggests that Lear wrote his nonsense to escape from his fears and "haunting inhibitions" (27). She draws attention to the unappreciative "they" and to the fact that Lear's nonsense ridicules "the harshness of society" (27). Furthermore, she suggests that the nonsense reflects Lear's sense of his own ugliness or awkwardness. And like others Richardson also speaks of the later poems as being among the most compelling, for although the limericks offer "glimpses" of Lear's private life, these other poems take the reader much closer to it. After speaking briefly of Lear's love of words, Richardson concludes by comparing Carroll and Lear. For her the difference between the two nonsense writers is in their approach to their writing. Carroll "approaches his nonsense by way of logic and mathematics"; Lear, through his painting and poetry (36).

The second biography to be published is Vivien Noakes's *Edward Lear: The Life of a Wanderer* (1968). It is actually the first that may be considered authoritative. In meticulous detail, Noakes discusses the circumstances under which Lear first composed his nonsense verses. Through her narrative of his life, Noakes places these verses within the context of Lear's experiences and his attitudes toward himself. She suggests that Lear wrote not only for children, in whom he found tolerance, affection, and liveliness, but also for adults who having known loneliness and isolation more fully comprehended his poems. Throughout Noakes uses Lear's nonsense drawings as a sort of marginalia — as an ironic commentary upon the life and as a reminder to her readers that Lear's marvelous absurdity and feeling for nonsense was present, even during the worst of times.

In addition to placing Lear's nonsense within the context of his biography, Noakes discusses the work itself. She suggests that the nonsense in his verses emerges from the incongruous mixing of the "predictable, stable elements such as numbers, choruses, alliteration" with the unpredictable characters and situations Lear places before the reader (231). This paradox of the predictable and the unpredictable is essential. Like Sewell, she also asserts that a sense of detachment is basic. With these principles in mind, Noakes organizes Lear's nonsense writing into three overlapping groups: 1) the happy and inconsequential pieces, 2) the stories, and 3) those in which the sense of detachment breaks down because Lear's unhappiness starts to overwhelm the experience of nonsense.

Noakes's vividly written biography encouraged what was already a growing interest in Lear's nonsense so that during the 1970s there were even more publications and responses to his verses and stories than in the previous decades. One indication of the greater seriousness with which people regarded Lear is the fact that a collection of his original and unpublished nonsense drawings came up for auction at Christie's and commanded a price of £21,000. Frank Davis in his article "Putting a High Price on Nonsense" for *Country Life* mentions the sale. Still, he is one person who seems less impressed than most by Lear's work. He refers to Lear as "the little man" and speaks of his nonsense drawings as being "not very good" — merely "fine nursery stuff" (118). A similar attitude pervades another short piece on Lear in the same magazine. In the May 17, 1979, issue, the writer, perhaps the same one as above, refers to Lear as a "poor little man" who is "invariably irresistible even when not all of his Limericks are perfection ..." (1527).

The views expressed in *Country Life*, though, are obviously the exception. For the most part, critics were taking Lear's nonsense more and more seriously. Perhaps one of the most resolved of these critics is Dieter Petzold whose 1972 study of English nonsense in the nineteenth century (*Formen und Funktionen der englischen Nonsense-Dichtung im 19. Jahrhundert*) places Lear's nonsense within the English tradition of nonsense and deals, at length and with care — although without originality — with its reception in the nineteenth century. (For this reason his study can serve as a most helpful tool for those interested in surveying the history of nonsense.) For instance, he explains that Lear's nonsense depends upon the imagistic presentation of comic incongruity; that it lacks causality; it is full of non-sequiturs, language games, and sound sequences that seem to carry intelligible meaning. Petzold is also one of many critics to find that Lear's nonsense unconsciously belongs to Romanticism through its "poetry" and sense of romantic irony — his nonsense speaks of melancholy but undermines or undercuts the emotion through the very nature of its art. Petzold is also one of several to argue with Sewell's point that true nonsense bespeaks an emotional poverty. He argues that in Lear's nonsense there is emotion; there is a mood. He maintains that the limericks reveal suppressed anxieties. Even the drawings reveal some emotional uneasiness. For him the limericks' cheerfulness is always precarious because Lear's anxieties inevitably break through the laughter and affect the reader who cannot help but notice that the people in the limericks barely avoid suffering. (For additional commentary on this book, see chapter 2.)

When Sewell refused to entertain any psychological or Freudian analysis of Lear's nonsense, she must have been all too sensitive to that possibility. In the spring 1972 issue of *Unicorn: An Independent Miscellaneous Journal*, the inevitable happens. J. R. Christopher discusses the sexual imagery in "The Owl and the Pussycat." He traces the scrobic and phallic imagery in the poem. A year later (in the fall of 1973), Edmund Miller in "Two Approaches to Edward Lear's Nonsense Songs" (*The Victorian Newsletter*) also leaps into a rather simplistic Freudian reading of the nonsense poems. Miller maintains that the school which sees Lear's poetry as Romantic uncovers only part of what happens in the nonsense songs. Miller also sees the limericks and verses as expressions of Lear's "psychological peculiarities" (28). When Miller claims this, he is not writing about what critics often perceive — that the limericks present Lear as a person who is obsessively concerned with his nose, his beard, his eating habits, and his age — but is thinking rather specifically of Lear's sexual preoccupations. Using "The Pobble Who Has No Toes," "The Owl and the Pussy Cat," and "The Dong with a Luminous Nose," Miller remarks on the obvious phallic symbolism to make the point that the symbolism is present, but that Lear does not realize his own humor. I think Lear would not have been amused.

There are several major publications in the 1970s. One of these is *Lear in the Original: Drawings and Limericks by Edward Lear for his Book of Nonsense* (1975). The book has forty-eight drawings in pen and ink with limerick captions, illustrations by Lear for songs and poems composed by others, miscellaneous nonsense drawings, a few natural history drawings, and sketches that do not seem to be executed by Lear. In his introduction to this collection, Herman W. Liebert speaks of the limericks as being an escape for Lear. They are a "release" that enabled him "to endure" (13). Liebert emphasizes that Lear composed them "on the spur of the moment" and did not set out to write a book of nonsense. Liebert finds their resulting "freedom" delightful, for they "do not portray the restricting or boring world of grownups, where virtue and decorum rule and everything is in its place" (21). Lear, according to Liebert, stretched children's minds. He played with words and "made marvelously suggestive but meaningless words, a hundred years before James Joyce" (21).

In his introduction Liebert, naturally, writes about the drawings in the original album. He asks his readers to note the sharp contrast between Lear's nonsense drawings and his serious sketches and paintings. He proposes that Lear's nonsense drawings are "totally antithetical" to the serious work, for like the verses they accompany, they are "loose, free, imaginative, unconfined by perspective, and like the work of a gifted child." They have "none of the serenity" of his other work, for the figures are "full of action and emotion" (22). Throughout his introduction Liebert gives valuable information concerning the techniques of reproducing the drawings.

In the same year as *Lear in the Original* appeared, Brian Alderson's edition of Lear's selected nonsense, *A Book of Bosh*, also came out. It is intended to introduce Lear and his nonsense to children. In his introduction Alderson informs his young readers of the author's "rather melancholy life" (9) and of his "enormous energy" — his "hurried, boshy life" (12). Alderson notes that "there is an undertow of fear and sadness" in the nonsense songs. Lear's playing with language is, Alderson suggests, sometimes "a kind of defense, a refusal to show that he was lonely or frightened, or that he felt himself out of his depth in high Victorian society" (12-13). At the end of his book, Alderson adds a section he entitles "Wurbl Inventions" in which he gathers a group of Lear's invented words, such as "ombliverous."

Two years later, in 1977, John Lehmann's profusely illustrated book, *Edward Lear and his World*, appeared. His discussion of the nonsense writing begins with a brief history of the publication of the nonsense books. He then looks at the verses themselves to identify the various skills Lear employed. Lehmann isolates characteristics that one often reads about. For instance, he remarks upon Lear's adaptation of the limerick form, and he pays attention to the infamous "they" of the limericks. With respect to the "they," Lehmann writes, "Most of the time they are censorious, conventional and vindictive, interfering in innocent pleasures if they are in the least unusual." He continues, "One cannot help feeling that in these limericks Lear is giving vent to contempt and disgust for the officious, busybodying people through the violence with which he portrays their behaviour ..." (53). As if referring to Miller's article, Lehmann also points out the "unconscious phallic images" present in the nonsense.

Perhaps Lehmann's most significant contribution, though, is his commentary upon the nonsense drawings. He praises them for their "purity of line and free lyricism" (55); he notices the likeness between the people and the animals in the drawings; and, like Liebert, he points out how the nonsense drawings' "frenzy" differs from "the calm of Lear's watercolours" (56). Indeed, the difference is not difficult to see, for often the originals are more "grotesque" than the published versions. In the original the old man of Peru's wife grits her teeth and points toward the open oven with such determination that she suffers from none of the published drawing's vacuous and half-directed hostility. Lehmann's most striking observation about the drawings, however, is that the original ones are rougher, more violent and threatening, than the published versions. Using the preliminary and published drawings for the "old man of Peru," he concludes, "Sometimes, one feels, Lear may have had to keep a very close censorship on the emotions that welled up from his subconscious" (58). Like other critics before him, Lehmann also finds traces of Romanticism in Lear's nonsense, particularly in his longer poems. He sees these as a form of "transposed Romantic poetry, written with remarkable skill, with a sense of rhythmic architecture and word music that recalls the masters, especially his beloved Tennyson" (62).

An important critical event in 1977 is the publication of Thomas Byrom's *Nonsense and Wonder: The Poems and Cartoons of Edward Lear*. In this study of Lear's limericks, Byrom attempts something that no previous critic had thought of doing. He compares the limericks composed when Lear was in his twenties to the later ones written when he was in his fifties. On the surface, Byrom explains, the two sets appear to be similar, but a closer look, according to Byrom, reveals significant distinctions. By comparing the two sets Byrom finds that Lear embarked upon a search for a more peaceful and spiritual relationship to the world; consequently, in the second series "nature has become tamer and the beasts are more sociable, the music has grown more beneficent and death is a rare event, so also human relations have been transformed from the disastrous to the pacific" (106-7). Byrom, like others, also discusses the "they" of the limericks.

Perhaps the most interesting section in *Nonsense and Wonder* is the one in which Byrom discusses the discrepancies he notices between the pictures and the limericks they accompany. Sometimes these illustrations work "as an expansive complement" to the verses; at other times, they "refute what they are supposed to describe" (136). Generally speaking, though, these illustrations expand "the sense in the direction of a mysterious happiness at the expense of an intelligibly sensible, and often sensibly glum view of life" (138). Byrom closes by discussing the longer poems. Once more he concentrates upon the idea of wonder and places Lear within the tradition of the Romantic sublime.

It is only natural that Byrom's and Lehmann's books attracted reviewers' attention. Jonathan Cott's "How Interesting [rather than "pleasant"] to Know Mr. Lear" (*New York Times Book Review*, December 11, 1977) is one interesting example. It is notable for its "seventies" sensibility. In his review Cott claims that "Edward Lear is the first rock-and-roll poet." He explains:

> Just as Lear allowed Romanticism "to find a home away from home in the only underground available to high-minded Victorians — the world of children" (to quote Byrom), so rock-and-roll — unbeknownst to many children's books critics and librarians — has become the repository of some of our best children's literature: e.g., the Who's "Boris the Spider," the Beatles' "Yellow Submarine" and "Octopus's Garden." ... Songs like these owe much to Lear, as does the most Learian ... of all rock-and-roll songs, "I Am the Walrus" by the Beatles' John Lennon, who may be Edward Lear *redivivus.* (7)

In his review Cott indicates his desire to read a critic who "recognizes and respects" Lear as a "radical critic of sexual repression and bourgeois values" (36). He suggests that Lear's enduring popularity is due to that critical power.

Translations and adaptations are another mark of the increasing interest in Lear's writing. In 1973, for instance, there appeared a Hebrew translation of a selection of limericks and songs like "The Owl and the Pussy-Cat." In this publication the translator has made an attempt to imitate the rhythms as truly as possible. And in 1977 a German adaptation of Lear's nonsense came out. The author of this volume is the well-known poet Hans Magnus Enzensberger; the book's title is *Edward Lears Kampletter Nonsensins Deutsche geschmuggelt.* In this adaptation Enzensberger has "smuggled" Lear's limericks into German by transforming them into a Marxist criticism of oppressive or cruel German authority. He transforms the "they" of the limericks so that the verses become a satire on certain aspects of social and political behavior. Throughout Enzensberger retains Lear's original drawings.

When S. S. Prawer reviewed Enzensberger's book for the *Times Literary Supplement* (December 23, 1977), he remarked that although Enzensberger wanted to give "Germans a Lear for their times," he did not succeed, for his transformations of the limericks ruin the original verses' intentions and atmosphere. They eliminate much of the mystery. They show that Enzensberger does not sympathize with Lear's brand of nonsense. For instance he alters Lear's "runcible" hat to a "common topper." In addition Mr. Floppy Fly's "mumbian melody" becomes "no more than a song belted out at full force" ("ein Lied aus vollem Schlunde"), and the "ombliferous" person of Crete finds herself reduced to "a flirtatious old bag" ("die alte Kokotte aus Schleiz") (1497). Prawer is obviously outraged with the distortion of Lear's voice.

As if resurrecting Lear's original tone, the following year (1978) Garland Publishing Company brought out a facsimile of an early edition of *A Book of Nonsense.* In his brief introduction David L. Greene gives a short history of the first three editions. Greene has little to say about the limericks except that their humor depends on their incongruity. He also mentions that some have tried to find a deeper significance in a few of the limericks. He, however, thinks that the limericks do little more than appeal to "the harmless sadism of most children" (viii).

One of the most interesting articles concerning the "deeper significance" in Lear's limericks and poems to appear in the 1970s is Ina Rae Hark's "Edward Lear: Eccentricity and Victorian Angst." Hark asserts that Lear's nonsense reflects not only his life but also his age and its anxieties. Building upon the various discussions of the "they" and upon various critics' sensitivity to the social conflicts expressed in the limericks, Hark adds that in many of the limericks the verses' subjects "empathize with 'them' in their struggles to cope with ... bizarre individualities" (115). She concludes that Lear's is a "double-edged" nonsense which acknowledges both revolutionary and reactionary or conservative principles. This paradox creates a "dynamic tension" in his poetry which is both "conservative and revolutionary, resigned and angry, uniquely autobiographical and representatively Victorian, all at once" (121).

Lear's personal fears and obsessions are once more the subject in Stephen Prickett's *Victorian Fantasy* (1979). He thinks, as have others, of Lear as a "misfit" — a marginal figure who stands outside the boundaries of convention (sexually) and who feels oppressed by "the rigid rules demanded by the etiquette of his aristocratic employer's world" (115). Lear was a person "to whom nonsense happened" (127). This alienation, according to Prickett, informs all of his nonsense writing. With this orientation in mind, Prickett criticizes Noakes for dividing the nonsense writing into three groups (see p. 17). Prickett believes that such schematizing misrepresents Lear whose sense of marginality informed all his nonsense in varying degrees. Lear is never emotionally uninvolved — he is not "logical" like Carroll — so to describe the limericks as being "detached" in content and as displaying "pure nonsense" is not accurate. Prickett closes his discussion by suggesting that nonsense is akin to fantasy, for both "depend on laws as tightly structured as those of the 'real' world," and both invert their culture. He concludes that nonsense "is the most rigidly controlled of all forms of fantasy" (127).

The 1980s and on

As Lear moved closer to the center of Victorian studies in the 1980s, and as the importance of his art was recognized in the landmark Royal Academy Show of 1985, responses to his work increased in frequency. In the 1980s he is less the eccentric outsider and more one of the major figures in Victorian literature. His role as "master of nonsense" also endures. His being a classic of children's literature keeps his work before readers of all ages. Furthermore, his work continues to increase in value at auctions. For instance, a 1981 manuscript collection of a set of recently discovered drawings for his *A*

Book of Nonsense fetched £16,000 at Sotheby's. More recently a 1993 catalogue from a rare book dealer lists a single nonsense drawing as being worth $4,500.

As in previous decades new editions of his nonsense continue to be issued. In 1980, for example, the Metropolitan Museum of Art in New York published a facsimile of a rare colored edition of *A Book of Nonsense* that, according to its introduction, originally appeared around the 1870s. And in 1982 Allen Lane published *Bosh and Nonsense*. This book adds previously unpublished verses and illustrations to the *oeuvre*. These new items come from two sketch books containing seventy-nine illustrated limericks that were found among the Duncan family papers in Naughton House, Fife. The drawings in *Bosh and Nonsense* are reproduced in the same size as in the original sketchbook. This edition adds to Herman W. Liebert's *Lear in the Original* (1975).

Lear's increasing importance for Victorian studies results in three pieces of writing that are standard scholarly tools. The first is a chapter on Lear in Arthur Pollard's edition of *The New History of Literature: The Victorians* (1987) — in an earlier edition of this history Lear had not been included. The chapter is written by Gillian Avery who thinks of Lear as a "sad clown" and a poet who does not participate in Carroll's "ruthless rationality." She also makes the nice point that much of the "humour lies in the way the victims brush aside the disasters with bland composure" (294-95). The second is *A Concordance to the Complete Nonsense* compiled by Ann Kearns Lyons, Thomas R. Lyons, and Michael J. Preston in 1980 — a book difficult to use because it breaks up the limericks and verses, and the third is Ina Rae Hark's *Edward Lear* (1982) prepared for the Twayne English Author Series.

In Hark's helpful study of Lear's lifetime work, there is, naturally, a section devoted to his nonsense writing and drawing. As well as explaining the basics (e.g. the structural patterns of the limericks), Hark expands and classifies her treatment of the "they" that appeared in the 1978 issue of *Victorian Poetry* ("Edward Lear: Eccentricity and Victorian Angst"). She also emphasizes the fact that contrary to what may have been believed, Lear's eccentrics are not all harmless and sympathetic cranks; they can be "self-centered," "self-destructive," and "antisocial" (43). They reflect Lear's "morbid" personality. She also corrects what she perceives to be an oversimplification on the part of critics like Davidson, Orwell, and Chesterton, who have tended to think of the "they" as creating a "one-sided" conflict (30). Contrary to what these critics have asserted, Hark suggests that "the relationship between the individual and 'them' has several facets." She lists them:

1. "They" are hostile and quell the innocent individual.
2. "They" are hostile, but the individual quells them.

3. "They" are hostile, but the individual is culpable in provoking their anger.
4. "They" express a neutral interest which the individual rebuffs.
5. The manner in which the individual expresses his individuality pleases "them," and "they" extend approval.
6. The individual is in difficulty, and "they" try to help him, or vice versa. (30)

In this monograph Hark speaks of the Learian paradox — of the fact that there is a tension, a double-sidedness that combines, incongruously, such elements as mysticism and practicality or the individual's desire and society's conventions. These tensions create an "uncertainty" or an atmosphere of "unpredictability" within the limericks which can be at once "mystic expression of eccentricity" (45) and records of an almost obsessive concern for the everyday. Often this paradox accentuates the uncertainty of Lear's world. Hark explains:

Predictable patterns do run through the limericks, e.g. "they" will react hostilely to eccentricity, gluttons will be punished, but just as one becomes confident in making such associations, the poet throws in an exception to upset them. Such final unpredictability is at base very frightening. (51)

For Hark, then, the ambiguities can be not only the cause of the humor but also the occasion for fear.

Hark distinguishes between the limericks and the longer poems by pointing out that the poems begin rather than end, as the limericks often do, with catastrophe. In the poems the autobiographical elements are more visible than they are in the limericks. Both the limericks and the poems, however, constitute one body of work, for both reflect Lear's "nonsensical life." Hark makes it clear that knowing the life "helps one to decode the nonsense" (129). She does, though, suggest that the nonsense is enjoyable on its own. She writes, "Clearly it was the nonsense itself, quite divorced from its author, that captivated Victorian children and adults" (130). Lear's work was a welcome alternative to the prevalent didacticism in children's literature. Hark also remarks that Lear's nonsense and its "unpredictability" caught the imagination of adults who would recognize in it a "not so fanciful reflection of conditions in their own rapidly changing world" (132).

The whole question of Lear's place in children's literature captures various critics' attention. Elizabeth Sewell's "Nonsense Verse and the Child" (1980) (see chapter 2) and Brian Alderson's "Literary Criticism and Children's Books" (1980) are two examples. In his essay Alderson uses critics' reactions to Lear's "The Daddy Long-Legs and the Fly" to discuss the larger question of how to approach a piece of children's literature. He suggests that historically there have been three major groups: the Educationalists, the Utilitarians, and the Authoritarians. In all these groups the critics judge a work in terms of its success or failure in pleasing or educating a child. Alderson complains that there seems to be no external standard that exists beyond these groupings and beyond the tastes or expectations of a particular time in history.

In the 1980s the old question of how Lear and Carroll compare continues to surface. It rises again in Gary Willis's "Two Different Kettles of Talking Fish: The Nonsense of Lear and Carroll." After acknowledging their similarities, such as the play with "meaningless" words and the creation of eccentric characters who move in a world which is always in flux, Willis focuses on their differences. Contrary to what many critics have already suggested, Willis thinks Lear greets "life with bland acceptance" (91); therefore, his nonsense retreats from deep feeling. It "does not exert the power over readers that Carroll's work does" (91). The most profound difference is that Lear's is a world in which innocence thrives. In contrast, Carroll's is one in which innocence is continually threatened by "malevolent predators" (89). Willis is uncomfortable with what he perceives to be Lear's universal tolerance of people — perhaps if he were to read Lear's correspondence and journals with its grumblings and criticisms of all sorts of individuals, Willis would alter his opinion.

Throughout the history of responses to Lear's limericks, the subject of its origins, history, and form has always been present. Lear's statement concerning his indebtedness to *The History of Sixteen Wonderful Old Women* (ca. 1821) or *Anecdotes and Adventures of Fifteen Gentlemen* (ca. 1882) and especially to "There was a sick man of Tobago" often gets reiterated as does his habit of varying the early limerick form by almost repeating the words of the first line in the last, a practice that some critics have found to be a weakness in his limerick writing, though most have defended it, and do not miss the traditional punch line. As to the origin of the limerick form, few critics attempt to inquire into it. Most are content either to identify the nursery rhyme or ballad tradition as appropriate models or to repeat the truism that the limerick's provenance is "uncertain." Yet others revert to the definition offered by J. H. Murray in the *Oxford English Dictionary* and think of the limerick as being derived from a custom at convivial parties, at which each member sang an extemporized nonsense verse that was followed by a chorus containing the words, "Will you come up to Limerick?" Still others, like Langford Reed who collected "clean" limericks, speculate that the form was brought to Ireland and anglicized by Irish mercenaries in the late seventeenth and early eighteenth centuries. And then there are others, like William S.

Baring-Gould, who remind readers that the limerick is originally a dirty, lewd, or scurrilous form. This is a perspective that helps color Gershon Legman's attitude toward Lear's limericks. In his introduction to the 1970 edition of *The Limerick* (it first came out in 1953), Legman writes that he detects in Lear's limericks an "insurmountable private fear of public disgrace (the only passions of his life being, unfortunately, for cats and handsome Greek boys)." For Legman, then, Lear's limericks are not really exceptions to the rule that the limerick is an indecent form. Although nothing indecent lies on the surface, "the verses are still indecent as unconscious revelations of obscenities in his life" (Belknap, 17).

In "The History of the Limerick" (1981) George N. Belknap studies the form's origins; he treats it as a literary genre in its own right, not only in the context of Lear's work. Belknap discusses Rudyard Kipling's, Aubrey Beardsley's, Susan Hale's, Andre Domin's, James Joyce's, and Edward Gorey's limericks. He also examines closely the various claims about its Irish origins and points out the various errors in other scholars' attempts to locate its beginnings. Unlike those who immediately jump to "There was a sick man of Tobago," Belknap suggests that James Clarence Mangan, the nineteenth-century Irish poet, is the source. Belknap believes that it is Mangan's "unorthodox anapestic limericks" that served as models for Lear. The form, then, from his point of view is not a distinctly English one. Belknap also argues that "if the responsible evidence that has been so far assembled can be trusted, the earliest published examples of the modern anapestic limerick appeared in 1820 and the name first appeared in print in 1898." Lear, it should be noted, did not refer to his early nonsense verses as limericks. He brought attention to the form, but he never used the name.

Another essay on the limerick form is William Harmon's "Lear, Limericks, and Some Other Verse Forms" (1982). Harmon argues that Lear neither invented nor perfected the limerick. Using the limericks from *The History of Sixteen Wonderful Old Women* and *Anecdotes and Adventures of Fifteen Gentlemen* as models of the "true limerick," Harmon explains how much Lear's verses deviate formally from these. He proposes that it would be more accurate to refer to Lear's nonsense limericks as "nonsenses" — the term Lear used. Perhaps because Harmon considers Lear's limericks to be formally false, he also finds them inferior to the longer poems and songs. It is in these later pieces that Harmon finds Lear's "greatness." Harmon concludes his essay by mentioning two other verse forms that he believes are other variations of the true limerick: the clerihew and the double dactyl.

Yet another essay is Wim Tigges's "The Limerick: The Sonnet of Nonsense" (1987) which surveys the various attitudes toward what a limerick should or should not be and discusses why it is an appropriate medium "for conveying nonsensical messages" (118). Tigges also makes the interesting suggestion that the limerick, like the sonnet, works better within a sequence than on its own — it comes closer to the idea of nonsense. Tigges explains:

> The effect of a sequence upon the reader is not only that of offering a particular feeling or event from various angles; it also suggests the presence of infinity .... In a sequence, then, both the sonnet and the limerick lose their individual limitedness. As one poet wishes to tell his beloved over and over again that his love is infinite and eternal, so the other presses upon us the infinity and eternity of the incomprehensibility of existence, of the struggle between individual and society, or simply of the sordidness of the "bottom" part of life. (132)

Tigges, of course, recognizes that the analogy between the limerick and the sonnet is not without its difficulties.

In 1988 the history of Lear's limericks also receives close attention with the publication of *Nonsensus*, a book which compares the text of all 116 published limericks included in the first three editions of *A Book of Nonsense*. The concern of the compiler, Justin G. Schiller, is to record variations in Lear's own language in these three editions. In addition Schiller offers a census of known copies of the true first edition, describes the various manuscripts of these early limericks, identifies their provenance, and offers a probable reconstruction of the limericks' original order.

Another sort of census appears in a 1985 issue of *Literary Onomastics Studies*. Here Priscilla A. Ord in "'There Was an Old Derry Down Derry, Who Loved to Make Little Folks Merry:' A Closer Look at the Limericks of Edward Lear" counts the number of place names, rhyme words, adjectives, and topographical features in the limericks.

As is obvious, perhaps, from the above discussion, the limericks seem to command more attention in the 1980s than in the previous decades. Furthermore, they command a different sort of attention, for in the 1980s the limericks also become the occasion for theoretical rather than biographical, descriptive, or historical essays.

The first of these more theoretical treatments of Lear's nonsense is Paul Bouissac's "The Meaning of Nonsense (Structural Analysis of Clown Performance and Limericks)" (1982). In this rather confusing essay Bouissac speaks of two of Lear's limericks, "There was an Old Person of Dover" and "There was an Old Man in a tree," as "meta-cultural" phenomena (200). They are discourses that reflect a "fundamental dichotomy between culture and nature" (211). In the course of his argument, Bouissac emphasizes, as does Hark, the major themes in the limericks, especially the attention Lear gives to the act of eating or, as he would say, to the "culture's culinary code."

A second example of these more theoretical essays is Gioiella Bruni Roccia's "Il Problema del Testo Nel *Book of Nonsense* di Edward Lear" in *Studi Italiani di Linguistica Teorica ed Applicata* (1985). This is a most suggestive and original article that examines a single limerick ("There was an Old Man with a beard") in order to explore the identification between the human and the animal world and to expose the resulting dialectical tension. In the process of analyzing this limerick, Bruni Roccia identifies the various phases a reader goes through while responding to the text. These six phases are: the pre-textual phase in which Lear's work appears to be not even a text — it is merely "an unstructured series of semantic incongruities" (273); the metaphoric phase in which the reader sees a simple story line; the nonsense phase in which the reader recognizes the implicit incongruities within the story or between the verse and the illustration; the resolving phase in which the reader resolves the limerick's ambiguities and through that activity finds a way to interpret or discover a motivation for the limerick; and, finally, a topological phase in which the reader finds a more general topic to pull the various parts (the micro-texts) together.

One of the key phrases within this article is "nonsense nuclei." This is a term Bruni Roccia uses to describe the moments or the points at which the nonsense (rather than the sense) makes itself known. In "There was an Old Man with a beard," one of those nuclei occurs when the text announces that the old man expects the birds to nest in his beard — when he exclaims "just as I feared." This fear or expectation, according to Bruni Roccia, does not belong to the "real" world of sense; therefore, it is the point at which the nonsense shows itself. In her discussion Bruni Roccia also makes perceptive and refreshing remarks about the relationship between the verses and their illustrations. She is, for instance, intrigued by the figures' arm positions and what they reveal.

Bruni Roccia's article is, by the way, an example of the continuing interest in Lear by non-English speaking scholars. Other articles to be published in the 1980s are, for instance, Aldo Vittorio Grassi's "L'universo nonsensico dei 'limerick' di Edward Lear" (1986) and Rostyslav Dotsenko's ["Journey to the Land of Contrariety"]. The latter essay is from the Ukraine. Dotsenko wonders at the fact that in such "a reserved, logical nation" as England, a figure like Lear would emerge. Lear himself, the author adds, also exhibited many paradoxes. For instance, "he was sickly yet unbelievably industrious." The limericks too are examples of this "world of contrariety" (188–89). Dotsenko closes the article by remarking upon how frequently Lear has been translated. One recent translation is into Ukrainian. It is a collection of "fables" translated by O. Mokrovols'kyi and published in 1980.

Another theoretical article is Ann C. Colley's "The Limerick and the Space of Metaphor" (1988). Referring to the literalizing tendency in Lear's limericks, Colley points out that these nonsense verses do more than expose and play with the foibles of humanity; they also, perhaps surprisingly, parody the metaphoric impulse and in so doing afford a view of metaphor which might otherwise be unavailable. Colley explains, "Nonsense strips metaphor of its normal context and reveals the visible and audible spaces which define its structure and which are the source of its power" (66). The limericks are, therefore "accidental" commentators on metaphor. By literalizing it, they bring the metaphor's intrinsic character to the surface. Colley explains:

> To begin with, they [the limericks] expose the first phase of metaphor — the moment involving the anxiety of difference. The puzzling and slightly worrisome associations involved in the limericks parody the unusual conjunctions within the metaphoric comparison which unbalance the reader, and, initially cause him to be primarily aware of the dissimilarities between the object and what is being identified through it. For instance, the bringing together of the carp and the harp ("The Young Lady of Welling"), a hatchet and a flea ("An Old Man of the Dee"), and a smile and voyage on a goose's back ("The Old Man of Dunluce") echoes and exaggerates the more memorable metaphoric conjunctions (e.g., the compass and love in Donne's "A Valediction Forbidding Mourning"). Moreover, the limericks seem to participate in the second phase of metaphor — the resolution of the differences into similarities and congruity. The concluding metaphoric adjectives mock the reader's impulse to find a resting place in congruity, and in that act remind him of the ever-present audible and visible spaces within metaphor itself. (70)

Using these observations, Colley then goes on to discuss the nature of metaphor in Ovid and Dante. The paradigm that the limericks unconsciously offer enables her to look freshly at the use of metaphor in *The Metamorphoses* and *The Divine Comedy*. At the conclusion of her article, she returns to an examination of Lear's limericks. She suggests that "the pleasure of the limericks is that their hyperbolic and parodic modes exaggerate and widen the spaces the metaphor admits and let the reader play safely among them" (87). She concludes, "The power of the limerick seems, finally, to derive from the spaces provided by the metaphoric vehicle" (88).

Important articles on the relationship between Lear's limericks and their illustrations appeared in 1987 and 1988. Lisa Ede's "Edward Lear's Limericks and Their Illustrations" was published in a collection of essays entitled *Explorations in the Field of Nonsense* (1987). In this essay, Ede states that the richness of Lear's limericks emerges not so much from their words as from their illustrations. She addresses the matter of the complex relationship between the verses and their pictures. It is, she asserts, this relationship which creates the meaning to be found in the limericks. Like Byrom she observes that the illustrations often contradict the verses. This contradiction increases the limericks' sense of ambiguity. Ede also points out that the illustrations help clarify and sharpen "the anti-social attitude which is often only implied in the verse" (113). In the same volume of essays, Hedrik van Leeuwen in "The Liaison of Visual and Written Nonsense" asks the question, "How large is the influence of the illustration on the text?" and speaks more generally about the experience of visual art as being one in which there is no development — the figures are frozen in movement. Therefore, the visual art's "meaning" is determined more intuitively than the understanding that comes from language.

Ann C. Colley's "Edward Lear's Limericks and the Reversals of Nonsense" is also about Lear's illustrations. In this article, written for an issue of *Victorian Poetry* to honor Edward Lear (1988), Colley discusses the relationship between the drawings executed for the nonsense verses and the landscape paintings Lear produced for a living. The incongruities between Lear's humorous pieces and his earnest work are significant, for no correspondence between the two styles easily avails itself. According to Colley, these incongruities need not be alienating. Rather, their dissimilarity helps explicate the topsy-turvy mode of nonsense and, in particular, makes it possible to regard Lear's limericks not only as antitheses of the serious pieces but also as inversions of them. In a sense the limericks emerge as reverse images of Lear's paintings: Lear's informal way of composing his nonsense reverses his diligent and elaborate approach to his academic paintings; the limericks displace and twist the realism of these paintings by stretching, approximating, and exaggerating the idiosyncracies and implications of the serious compositions; in addition, the limericks reverse the paintings by pushing aside associations, eradicating shadows and images, and expelling superfluous dimensions; the limericks also negate the sense of time that the landscapes and oils attempt to portray; they also reverse the serious work by opening up what the topographies and prints enclose. In the limericks, the faces of the subjects "turn to look out beyond the text" and "frolic on a frameless page" (291).

In the 1990s two critics, at least, have chosen to discuss Lear's nonsense within its social context — a reflection, perhaps, of the increasing interest in literature and cultural studies. They point the way, perhaps, to more work in this area. Ina Rae Hark's "The Jew as Victorian Cultural Signifier: Illustrated by Edward Lear" (1990) is one of the two. In this article Hark examines the caricatures of Jews in Lear's writings and drawings to demonstrate how paradoxical his attitudes were. He was capable of conforming to the Victorian stereotypes; he could call up the conventional comic caricatures; he could see Jews as "exotics"; and, at the same time, he could hold them up as "a refreshing contrast to the foibles of Christianity"; he could value them as patrons and friends, and think of them as "a noble and gifted people often unjustly maligned by the ignorant and persecuted by the zealot" (86). According to Hark, this ambiguity results from Lear's own marginal relationship to the dominant Victorian cultural ideology; at the same time, he shares the nonconformist impulse of nonsensical discourse that is acutely aware of the "they," the voice of the dominant cultural ideology. A second article is Ann C. Colley's "Edward Lear's Anti-Colonial Bestiary" which appeared in *Victorian Poetry* (1992). In this essay Colley talks about Lear's relationship to an imperialistic culture and his tendency to criticize its treatment of animals — its impulse to colonize the animal world. Lear used his drawings that accompanied his limericks to register his criticism. The result is that Colley discovers a "political" agenda in these limericks. They have a historical background that one does not usually think of attaching to Lear's work. Lear's nonsense, she concludes, is not as exclusively full of "wonder" or as free of immediate purpose as Byrom or anyone who enjoys the limericks entirely for their fun might believe. (For a fuller treatment of this article, see chapter 3.)

Like the Young Lady of Ryde, Lear's nonsense with its unquenchable humor will always attract attention. Like the "small spotty dogs" who bounce gaily about her, the critics will gather around the nonsense and what they write, like the young lady's umbrella that is both too small and just a little off target, will fail to contain or "cover" the nonsense. There will always be some part that eludes analysis. Perhaps that is one reason that critics have hardly ever attempted to place the limericks, the songs, and the stories within either the old or the current schools of criticism.

Undoubtedly there will be more criticism to come. Not only is Lear now an established figure; he is also very much alive in people's imagination. Children, like a nine-year old I know, still respond to his verses and shorten lengthy car rides by reciting "There was an Old Man who said 'Hush!'" And readers of the *New Yorker* easily recognize the figures on Ronald Searle's untitled July 27, 1992 cover showing the owl and the pussycat afloat, but this time in Central Park.

2: Lear and Nonsense Theory

> *Okul scratchabibblebongibo, viddle squibble*
> *tog-a-tog, ferrymoyassity amsky flamsky*
> *ramsky damsky crocklefether squiggs.*

SOME OF THE MOST significant critical reactions to Edward Lear's work can be found in the theoretical writing about nonsense. From the moment they first appeared, Lear's verses and stories along with those of Lewis Carroll stimulated an interest in the question, "What is nonsense?" Even though, of course, there was already a tradition of nonsense writing — Lear and Carroll certainly did not invent the genre — the popularity of these two writers within their own lifetime caused critics to take a closer look at it. Since then their writings have continued to be the occasion for considering the nature of nonsense. In this respect when critics refer to Lear, as "the father of nonsense," they are being more accurate than they, perhaps, realize, for Lear not only legitimized or popularized the genre; he also provoked readers to take a closer, more analytical look at it.

Although Carroll's work has generally attracted a more philosophical criticism, Lear's has invited serious and interesting responses. In this chapter I have selected studies of nonsense that use Lear's writing to formulate or approach an understanding of what nonsense is. I have not, therefore, included such works as Gilles Deleuze's *Logique du sens* (1979), for it refers exclusively to Carroll's nonsense. I have chosen, rather, many of the major and a few of the less recognized theoretical studies in which Lear's nonsense plays a significant role. Obviously some of the works discussed in the previous chapter appear again in this one. It is, of course, only natural that critics who have looked carefully at Lear's work have also wanted to engage the larger subject. The consequent overlapping is to be expected.

Inevitably a review of theories about nonsense reveals that similar ideas get reiterated yet within different contexts. One way in which a review of the critical literature can be helpful is by allowing the reader to become more sensitive to these recurring themes. A chronological summary such as the one that follows, however, runs the risk of overwhelming the reader, so before beginning the survey, it is, perhaps, necessary to identify these threads of thought that help pattern the critics' various theories.

As might be expected, many critics refer to the role of language and everyday objects within the genre. They often speak of nonsense as a "game" and enumerate the numerous ways of playing with words and things. Within these limits or according to the game's rules, nonsense, although it seems to be illogical, has its own idea of order. Others prefer to think of nonsense as "pure and absolute" — it is to be enjoyed for its own sake; it is neither threatening nor painful. And as such it offers an escape from a controlling culture and the limitations of its author. Others, however, understand that nonsense can participate in difficult and painful matters, for it can reveal anxieties and can cause the reader to recognize them within himself. Nonsense is not, therefore, necessarily a detached or non-sentimental idiom. For still other critics nonsense is very much a social phenomenon that exposes the culture it manipulates. Naturally many critics also speak of the "topsyturvydom" of nonsense and dwell upon its incongruities. They also identify the tensions that result from the fact that nonsense lies somewhere between sense and no sense, rules and anarchy, plausibility and implausibility.

A number of critics also approach the genre by thinking of it as a "fine art" — as a significant literary form. Within this context, some, as we have seen, consider Lear's nonsense, especially, to be "poetic" and link his work, for instance, to Tennyson's. The question of how nonsense relates to wit, humor, and laughter arises, and so does the significant specter of nationalism — the "Englishness" of nonsense. The relationship of the child to nonsense is another recurring concern. There are also those critics who find within it a kind of spirituality and transcendence. They claim that through its repatterning of reality, nonsense leads the reader to other modes of thought. As the following survey will begin to suggest, the field of nonsense is large and often ambiguous. It situates itself somewhere between word games and metaphysics, escape and attachment, incongruity and order, a universal form and a historically specific phenomenon.

The Nineteenth Century

The publication of Lear's nonsense books almost immediately drew attention to the question, "What is nonsense?" Their popularity (for instance, *A Book of Nonsense* first published in 1846 was in its twenty-sixth edition in 1888) "fixed the name of nonsense" (*The Quarterly Review*, 1888, 358) and caused critics to try to identify the characteristics of what was giving them and so many other readers such pleasure.

An 1887 reviewer for *The Spectator* is eager to distinguish nonsense, particularly Lear's, from the inferior work of the fashionable punsters and satirists with "ulterior motives." The reviewer believes, as many critics after him have believed, that nonsense is not dependent upon time or place. It is itself — "pure and absolute" (493). This belief that nonsense has no symbolic meaning and is apolitical helps structure Sir Edmund Strachey's article entitled "Nonsense as a Fine Art" (*The Quarterly Review*, 1888). In this essay Strachey begins by speaking of nonsense as "the proper contrary to sense." With the help of that basic opposition he then isolates the genre's various characteristics: that nonsense uncovers the "incongruities of all things within and without us" (335); that in addition to bringing forward such absurdities, nonsense uncovers "a new and deeper harmony of life in and through its contradictions"; and that nonsense is not "painful" — its surprises and its way of allowing the reader to see things "so out of place" are a source of delight rather than discomfort. Strachey is also quick to distinguish it, especially Lear's, from vulgar eighteenth-century parodies. He prefers to identify nonsense as a "fine art," — as the "flower and fruit of Wit and Humour" — so he spends several pages narrating its history, from Chaucer to Charles Lamb, and concludes by discussing Lear's verses and poems. Strachey's is probably one of the first systematic attempts to describe literary nonsense and, consequently, it sets the tone for many subsequent discussions. Strachey also introduces two other familiar themes that recur in later pieces of criticism: the notion that nonsense brings confusion to order and, as a result, sets the world upside down ("topsyturvydom") and the understanding that to have nonsense there must be an absence of emotional involvement — an attitude that colors discussions of nonsense in the 1950s and after.

A month later a reviewer in the November 3 issue of *The Spectator* commented upon *The Quarterly Review* essay by suggesting that nonsense is not necessarily the "flower and fruit of wit and humour" and that "good" nonsense "must have the ring of sincerity about it" (1505). This reaction to Strachey's article is interesting, though, not so much because it argues with his belief that nonsense is "the inevitable concomitant of a keen wit or a strong sense of humour" (1504) but because it also insists that nonsense is a national phenomenon. The reviewer wonders, for instance, "What would a Frenchman make of" nonsense? In his mind the Germans, the French, the Americans, and the English each possess these idiosyncratic modes of nonsense. The point is, however, that the English nonsense is superior to all others, that the English, especially, "worship" or appreciate it. This opinion persists throughout the nineteenth and twentieth centuries.

There were, of course, critics in the nineteenth century who approached nonsense from other perspectives. Some of these preferred to think of its psychological dimensions. For instance, a reviewer for the November 10, 1894, issue of *The Spectator* defines the genre by considering the conditions under which it emerges. The "best" nonsense, he believes, comes from those moments of relaxation that occur between times of stress. He writes, "Nevertheless, we do not believe that Nonsense is ever at its best unless there be some real strain upon the mind from which there are seasons of relaxation" (639). He continues by making the interesting suggestion that it is a form that can only be properly written "in the intervals of freedom between times of sharp strain." In his acutely metaphoric style he adds, "Nonsense is the rebound when the bow is unstrung; but a bow that has never been strung cannot be unstrung" (639). That is to say, without some form of stress there can be no nonsense.

The Early Twentieth Century

The lasting popularity of Lear's nonsense verses and stories continued to motivate people to think about nonsense. One of the earliest of such studies is G. K. Chesterton's "A Defence of Nonsense" (1901). In this essay, Chesterton regards the modern nonsense, Lear's particularly, as possessing absolutely no meaning, for it is neither satirical nor parodic, as is that of Aristophanes, Rabelais, and Sterne. He suggests that "no age except our own could have understood that the Quangle-Wangle meant absolutely nothing, and the Lands of the Jumblies were absolutely nowhere." He explains:

> We fancy that if the account of the Knave's trial in *Alice in Wonderland* had been published in the seventeenth century it would have been bracketed with Bunyan's *Trial of Faithful* as a parody on the State prosecutions of the time. We fancy that if *The Dong with the Luminous Nose* had appeared in the same period every one would have called it a dull satire on Oliver Cromwell. (124)

Chesterton, though, does more than speak of contemporary nonsense as an apolitical genre. He also isolates two of its other primary characteristics. The first is that it offers an avenue of escape. It takes the reader and the writer into "a world where things are not fixed horribly in an eternal appropriateness" (124). It places them in a landscape where apples grow on pear trees and "any odd man you meet may have three legs" (124). The second characteristic reflects Chesterton's own religious preoccupations. Nonsense, he believes, is more than an aesthetic fancy; it is also a "spiritual" impulse, for it aids "the spiritual view of things" by causing its reader to "exult in the 'wonders' of creation" (126) — an observation that Thomas Byrom in the

1970s explores more systematically in his *Nonsense and Wonder*. By marveling at the shapes of things and at their unreasonableness, nonsense, Chesterton suggests, shares a foundation with or parallels the experience of spirituality. He writes:

> Nonsense and faith (strange as the conjunction may seem) are the two supreme symbolic assertions of the truth that to draw out the soul of things with a syllogism is as impossible as to draw out Leviathan with a hook.

He concludes, "Nonsense is faith" (127).

Another important study of the subject in these early years is Emile Cammaerts's *The Poetry of Nonsense* (1925). Cammaerts opens his investigation by remarking that even though nonsense is an old literary form, it is one that "has not received all the attention it deserves" (2). (Indeed his book is a corrective, for it is the first full-length study to isolate and describe some of the techniques peculiar to the genre.) Cammaerts proceeds by pointing out that it is in Lear's work that one discovers the "true characteristics" of nonsense. Like many critics before and after him, Cammaerts distinguishes nonsense from wit and satire and insists upon its purity and simplicity. Speaking of Lear's limericks, for instance, he remarks that

> They do not contain any sparkling witticism or any striking caricature, still less any worldly wisdom. They are just sheer nonsense, and, unless we enjoy nonsense for nonsense's sake, we shall never be able to appreciate them. (7)

Not content to remain with this truism Cammaerts attempts to find more specific answers to the question, "What is nonsense as a literary genre?" As he admits, he finds it easier to answer his question by enumerating what nonsense is not: it is not epigram; it is not satire, for it has no allusions to current events; it is not entirely a play on words; it is not a parody because nonsense is essentially "meaningless"; it does not tell a connected story — indeed the main purpose is to upset all logic; it is not magical — it is not to be confused with a fairy tale; and it is not an expression of sentimental humor. Through this series of negatives, Cammaerts evolves an understanding that nonsense is without meaning — that is, it confuses convention and logic and in so doing recovers the child's opposition to the dictates of reason. It records "the hostility to the well-ordered world to which 'grown-ups' vainly endeavour to introduce" the child. Because nonsense functions this way, it offers comfort to the "sensible man." Most of all nonsense is restless and exciting. In an engaging and interesting analogy, Cammaerts describes this quality. He suggests that nonsense is:

> the wild, exuberant mood of a Christmas party or of a popular carnival in which every reveller loses his identity under his disguises and indulges in the most impossible pranks. It runs in all directions and gesticulates madly, just as children and young animals do when let loose in an open field, after a long confinement. (15–16)

Because Cammaerts concerns himself with nonsense as a literary form, he devotes a chapter to its techniques. He emphasizes that it requires considerable skill; it is not something one just dashes off, for there has to be "perfect harmony between the matter and the form" (40). The topsyturvydom of nonsense emerges from knowing and then turning upside down the "general laws of good poetry" (40). He points out an interesting paradox: even though the nonsense rhymes "misbehave," the rhythm of their verses is "much more docile and follows rules scrupulously" (52). Cammaerts also finds a "certain connection between the attitude of mind of the old and modern romanticists and the Nonsense-writers." He suggests that Lear and Carroll are similar to writers like Ruskin and Tennyson, for they "make the same appeal to the imagination; they rely on the picture more than on the word, and on sentiment more than on intellect" (85). Keeping this association in mind, he discovers a "great deal of music" in nonsense verse. Because nonsense is essentially "musical," it is "most poetical."

Perhaps one of the most suggestive points Cammaerts makes is that the meaning of nonsense "is intimately associated not with an idea but with an image" (10). Maybe it is because of this orientation that he devotes a full chapter to the relationship between nonsense verses and their illustrations. He remarks upon the tendency of nonsense writers to illustrate their texts and notices that illustrators who are not the original writers do not do justice to the nonsense. Illustrators tend to overlook "the grotesque abruptness inherent in nonsense" and ignore its "brutal innocence" (64–65).

The Poetry of Nonsense concludes with the familiar claim that the English temperament is predisposed to nonsense, that the nation's sense of "broad humour" and ability "to enjoy a joke even if there is no point in it" (74) leads to an appreciation of nonsense. Like the reviewers in the preceding century, he finds nothing comparable in either French or German culture.

In the 1930s there were a number of short articles on the subject. One of these, for instance, is Erika Leimert's 1937 essay, "Die Nonsense-Poesie von Edward Lear (Ein Beitrag zur Psychologie des englischen Humors)." This essay is part of a continuing exploration of nonsense theory on the part of German scholars. In her discussion Leimert places herself among the many, like Cammaerts, who find nonsense to be typically English, or, especially, Victorian, for it celebrates the eccentric outsider. According to Leimert, in that cultural context nonsense emerges as an amorphous blend of comedy, irrationality, and fantasy. Her perception is similar to Walter de la Mare's. Writing in 1932 de la Mare had spoken of nonsense as being an "indefinable cross" between humor, fantasy, and a sweet unreasonableness (8).

The 1950s

After Cammaerts's examination of the genre, the next major study based upon the writing of Lear and Carroll is Elizabeth Sewell's *The Field of Nonsense*, published in 1952. Almost predictably she opens her discussion by pitting nonsense against sense and by stating that nonsense is "a collection of words or events" which fail to conform to the conventional patterns of a language to which a particular mind is accustomed. Sewell builds upon this distinction by enumerating three ways in which the mind reacts to this phenomenon: 1) The mind dismisses nonsense for, like a dream, it fails to correspond to reality. 2) The mind enjoys nonsense for its annihilation of order and its disregard of rules. 3) The mind perceives that nonsense has its own structure "held together by valid mental relations" (4).

It is the last of these three reactions that Sewell develops in *The Field of Nonsense*. Her main point is that nonsense has its own logical structure. It is not "merely a denial of sense" — it has its own laws and constructs its own system. She explains:

> We are going to assume that Nonsense is not merely the denial of sense, a random reversal of ordinary experience and escape from the limitations of everyday life into a haphazard infinity, but is on the contrary a carefully limited world, controlled and directed by reason, a construction subject to its own laws. (5)

Using what she admits are often the disparate styles of Lear and Carroll, Sewell isolates the "laws of construction" that create nonsense. She begins with the premise that nonsense is a world of everyday things and, even more so, one of words. She writes, "In Nonsense all the world is paper and all the seas are ink" (17). The nonsense writer manipulates words as in a game played within "a limited field" and with "fixed rules." Sewell then explains that in this manner nonsense paradoxically is not devoted to disorder but is very much wedded to order. To support her point she notes the orderliness of Lear's and Carroll's minds.

Because nonsense is essentially an orderly language game, it demands rules. If the writer fails to follow them or steps beyond the game's enclosures, he finds himself "wandering off" into the world of dreams or fantasy.

Sewell emphasizes her conviction that nonsense does not belong to those subjective worlds. It is, rather, a product of the mind's engagement with a "serial order" — with lists of things and numbers. Such is Sewell's belief in this necessity that she speaks of "nonsense failure" (149). Nonsense fails when the writer loses his detachment and admits too much of himself (his emotions) into the work.

Because nonsense is serial and is, therefore, composed of lists of everyday particulars, everything within it is detached. Nothing in nonsense ever approaches fusion. To maintain this serial world, the writer employs various safeguards. For instance, he avoids the idea of Beauty because beauty invites fusion — the beholder cannot be indifferent in its presence, and loses the sense of detachment among the elements. Another safeguard is that the writer blocks the entrance to the world of fantasy — hence, the tendency of the writers to illustrate their own work (a practice, of course, already noted by Cammaerts). Images, Sewell claims, easily take the reader away from the nonsense, especially since dreams are "almost entirely visual" (111). To prevent this possibility the writer must either carefully supervise the drawings or do his own. He must illustrate according to the rules of the game.

The regulations of the nonsense game isolate its players so that the "one emotion permissible in Nonsense" (145) is the sense of isolation. Any other destroys nonsense. Sewell disagrees with Chesterton's equating nonsense with faith, for faith and its irrationality are outside the realm of nonsense and its enclosures. She concludes that true nonsense needs neither belief nor disbelief. She writes, "We do not have to believe in the Jumblies or the blackbirds in the pie. They are in the game, and that is enough" (185).

Two incidental points Sewell makes are worth noting. One is that nonsense has an "immense sense of balance and safety" (5). The second is that nonsense should not be confused with the humorous or the comic. Sewell believes that laughter is only incidental to nonsense.

In the 1950s, of course, a few articles on the subject of nonsense appear. One is Eric Partridge's essay on Lear in *Here, There and Everywhere: Essays Upon Language*. Not surprisingly because of his interest in language, Partridge treats nonsense as verbal play and describes its reliance upon neologisms, portmanteau words, and puns.

The 1960s and 1970s

Many of the critics in the 1960s and 1970s seem intent upon classifying the genre or cataloguing the elements that make nonsense a literary form. For instance, in 1962 Rolf Hildebrandt names three types of nonsense: 1) Volks-Nonsense (folk or popular nonsense), 2) ornamental nonsense (the various ways of playing with words), and 3) literary or "pure" nonsense (by this he means the classics like those written by Lear and Carroll). According to

Hildebrandt nonsense is simply a formal phenomenon, the principal purpose of which is playing with language without a particular goal or purpose and without any emotional engagement. All these qualities, he believes, are specifically English.

Another analytical work in the 1960s is Alfred Liede's ambitious *Dichtung als Spiel: Studien zur Unsinnspoesie an den Grenzen der Sprache* (1963). Liede surveys the history of playful literature. In the second volume he lists all the possible verbal devices and forms associated with nonsense, both literary and non-literary, and remarks on the kinds of nonsense associated with various nations and contexts. From his point of view, literary nonsense is a form of play with the given language which allows both writer and reader to flee from their learning (*Bildungsglaubigkist*) and enter the innocent, pure, and playful nonsense of the child. For Liede, though, nonsense is an inferior form of poetry; it is the work of a "weak poet."

One of the most comprehensive of these analytical studies is Dieter Petzold's *Formen und Funktionen der englischen Nonsense-Dichtung im 19. Jahrhundert* (1972). This book opens with an analysis of Lear's and Carroll's nonsense. Petzold then examines other nonsense writing in nineteenth-century England. In the third chapter he meticulously surveys the reception of literary nonsense in the Victorian period and concludes by discussing the form in twentieth-century Britain and Germany.

Although Petzold is more interested in addressing how others have reacted to or written about nonsense, he does offer his own response, but it turns out to be rather conventional. For example, in his analysis of Lear's and Carroll's work, Petzold carefully catalogues various and rehearsed characteristics of nonsense: its lack of causality; its pleasing freedom from logical thinking; its comic use of language; its interest in sounds and sequences that seem to carry intelligible meaning, and its linguistic surprises. Of more interest, though still familiar, is Petzold's suggestion that nonsense belongs unconsciously to Romanticism, specifically that it expresses a kind of romantic irony, for nonsense undermines a genuine response to the world around it. This observation, of course, extends the belief held by previous critics (see chapter 1) that Lear's poems are as "poetic" or as "musical" as those of the Romantic poets, and that Lear's sense of disjunction is theirs too.

Petzold disagrees, as others have done, with Sewell's belief that pure nonsense lacks emotion or that nonsense fails if it introduces an emotional element into its field. Petzold claims that nonsense poems and stories often have a "mood"; they are not merely comic. Furthermore, he suggests that even though its characters appear to be invulnerable, the nonsense itself often expresses suppressed anxieties. These anxieties break through so that the laughter "sticks in one's throat" and reminds readers of their own difficult experiences. The characters in nonsense only appear to be invulnerable.

Klaus Reichert's 1974 study of nonsense is another analytical work. Reichert concentrates upon English Victorian nonsense literature. He limits his discussion to Victorian examples not only because he wishes to concentrate upon Lear and Carroll but also because he believes that nonsense as its own genre cannot extend beyond that period. Reichert makes the interesting point that after the period beginning with Lear and ending with Carroll, nonsense is no longer needed, for it and its idiosyncracies have been absorbed into regular literature. Reichert suggests that twentieth-century literature has "caught up" with Victorian nonsense writing. In his book Reichert also isolates the main characteristic of nonsense: its sense of isolation, disintegration, and discontinuity. For him nonsense exists in the space between there being no sense and there not yet being any meaning.

Not all the work in these two decades, though, concerns itself with histories and surveys of nonsense. For instance, Donald J. Gray's 1966 article, "The Uses of Victorian Laughter," discusses the question of nineteenth-century nonsense within the larger context of the Victorian sense of humor. Using numerous examples from periodicals, entertainments, and poems, Gray points out the similarities between nonsense and other forms of Victorian humor. For instance, nonsense shares humor's incongruities, its references to everyday things and to ordinary life, and above all the playing with words and its "delight in the sound of words." Gray also illustrates how nonsense distinguishes itself from humor by creating the illusion of autonomy and by asserting its "rigorous control" (168). He explains:

> Consonance, integrity, its pretense to be complete and conventionally coherent: that is what makes nonsense. Like other entertainments which furnish release from the imperatives of ordinary experience, nonsense amuses by failing to achieve the coherence expected of sounds and sentences and literary forms like those it uses. But the writers of nonsense also amuse by being careful to make their poems and tales so coherent in their own terms that they seem to be making sense, so entire and satisfying in their logic and motion that their order seems to be free-standing and completely independent of the conventional order of language and literature against which they are in fact playing. (171–72)

Within this illusory frame, nonsense writers, according to Gray, "chose to consider death, pain, desolation, and other powerfully disruptive forces" (172). These writers, however, never ultimately confront these experiences; they only keep them "in view." Gray concludes by agreeing with Sewell that nonsense is like a game. He does seem to offer a corrective, though, when he emphasizes that "nonsense does end in laughter." For him laughter is not, as it was for Sewell, incidental.

A few critics in the 1970s place nonsense within its social context. For instance, Robert Benayoun in the introduction to his collection of nonsense, *Le nonsense* (1977), suggests that nonsense emerges with economic troubles and social injustice (10). He believes that, for instance, the difficulties that accompanied nineteenth-century industrialization are responsible for the creation of and popularity of nonsense in Victorian England. He is, as a result, sensitive to the anti-establishment nature of the genre.

The major theoretical study of nonsense within its social context is, though, Susan Stewart's *Nonsense: Aspects of Intertextuality in Folklore and Literature* (1978). In this book Stewart uses nineteenth-century nonsense as one of her models to propose a theory of nonsense. She asserts that nonsense is a social phenomenon. It has to be so because "discourse" or language is a social event. Nonsense and the process through which it comes into play depend upon the various "domains" of discourse and how they interact with one another.

One of the domains is that of common sense or reality. Every other domain outside this one modifies reality. Nonsense emerges from these transformations — the shifting from one domain to another; consequently, nonsense "will always be contingent upon the nature of the corresponding common sense" (51). Stewart explains this process by using the analogy of the differences between metonymy and metaphor. Realism, she claims, is metonymic, for it refers to a specific and recognizable context. Nonsense, however, is closer to metaphor, for the context is more amorphous — it has a multiplicity of messages. Metaphor, like nonsense, disrupts the conventional, accepted message. With this understanding, therefore, nonsense is "humor without context" (38). (For another study of nonsense and metaphor see Ann C. Colley's "The Limerick and the Space of Metaphor" [1988].)

In the second part of her study, Stewart classifies the processes that create nonsense. All of them emerge through a discourse with common sense. Many of these processes have already been recognized by other critics: reversal and inversions; play with boundaries of meaning and language; play with infinity (there is an infinity of possibilities in language); use of simultaneity (e.g. the pun); and arrangement and rearrangement within a closed field. All these are accomplished within the spirit of "play" — within "the contextual parameters of the playground" (199). In many ways, then, Stewart's book builds upon Sewell's 1952 *The Field of Nonsense*.

The 1980s and On

The interest in theories of nonsense continues in the 1980s and 1990s. As before critics use Lear's verses and stories to help them think about their subject.

In 1980-81 Elizabeth Sewell once more addresses the question of nonsense. In "Nonsense Verse and the Child," she suggests that the delight in nonsense is not necessarily indebted to the idea of disorder. As if revising her earlier work in *The Field of Nonsense* (1952), she states that what particularly attracts a child to nonsense is its "beauty." (In her earlier work Sewell had outlawed the idea of Beauty from nonsense.) Limiting herself primarily to Lear's work, especially to his interest in art and aesthetics, and using Benjamin Whorf's idea that one re-patterns the familiar in order to perceive new and "higher orders," Sewell proposes that nonsense also re-patterns letters and objects. Through that dislocation nonsense offers glimpses of "other orders beyond and through our usual perspectives. Nonsense may give delight in proportion as it makes possible such glimpses." The "glimpses" offered by Lear's nonsense are into the world of beauty. She concludes, "Nonsense may prove to be one of the child's roads to Beauty" (45).

Another example of the continuing interest in using Lear's work to discuss nonsense theory is Paul Bouissac's article "The Meaning of Nonsense (Structural Analysis of Clown Performances and Limericks)" in *The Logic of Culture: Advances in Structural Theory and Methods* (1982). Bouissac's hypothesis is that limericks and clown performances are "meta-cultural phenomena"; that is to say they stand outside or above the dominant culture, and, therefore, they reflect and reveal that culture. From this perspective, nonsense is useful, for when

> it is impossible to describe adequately a system from within, the only way to engage in a metadiscourse, when the system to be described is the set of conditions for the "sensibility" of any discourse, is to produce a nonsensical discourse. (200)

With this principle in mind, Bouissac analyzes a well-known clown scenario ("the bee and the honey") and then turns to two of Lear's limericks: "There was an Old Man in a tree" and "There was an old person of Dover." Both the clown sequence and the limericks comment upon society's culinary code.

It is, perhaps, fitting to begin to conclude this summary of nonsense theory with Wim Tigges's *Explorations in the Field of Nonsense* (1987) and with his edition of a collection of essays, *An Anatomy of Literary Nonsense* (1988), for these are recent books that survey the subject thoroughly. In the 1987 collection of essays there are three that refer to Lear. One is Lisa Ede's "Edward Lear's Limericks and Their Illustrations," an essay discussed in the previous chapter; the second is also by Ede. In this piece, "An Introduction to the Nonsense Literature of Edward Lear and Lewis Carroll," Ede suggests that the problems of miscommunication are central to nonsense. Language, therefore, is both the subject and the means of nonsense. Ede also states that nonsense emerges from a constant interplay between various dichotomies, particularly those involving "illusion and reality and order and disorder." She explains that nonsense is:

> a self-reflexive verbal construction which functions through the manipulation of a series of internal and external tensions. The basic dichotomies involve illusion and reality and order and disorder, with such further contrasting pairs as fantasy and logic, imagination and reason, the child and the adult, the individual and society, words and their linguistic relations .... (57)

In other words, nonsense emerges from a carefully balanced tension between these various opposing entities. Within this balance, nonsense freely explores a wide range of emotions, ideas, and attitudes.

Ede concludes her essay by stating that nonsense constitutes a play world; therefore, play theory can provide a useful model "to clarify how the dialectic functions in nonsense" (58).

The third essay in this anthology is Tigges's "An Anatomy of Nonsense." Building upon Ede's assertion that nonsense emerges from a series of tensions, such as those that arise when logic and dream or reason and emotion come closer together than usual, Tigges attempts to map the anatomy of nonsense. He defines it as "a genre of narrative [he believes that nonsense must tell a story] which balances a multiplicity of meaning with a simultaneous absence of meaning. This balance is effected by playing with the rules of language, logic, prosody and representation" (27). The greater this tension between meaning and the absence of meaning, the more the verse or story invites the reader to participate in the act of interpretation and simultaneously avoids "the suggestion that there is a deeper meaning," the more pronounced is the nonsense. This tension, ambiguity, and frustration, rather than the subject matter, are what distinguishes nonsense from other forms of narrative art.

A year later Tigges published his *Anatomy of Nonsense* (1988), a book based upon the earlier collection of essays. It is a study that explores the various characteristics of nonsense and attempts to work its way through to a satisfactory definition of it. The book offers an extensive survey of others' opinions and a comprehensive bibliography. In the section on Lear, Tigges returns to the understanding that nonsense writing evolves from the tensions or conflict between meaning and absence of meaning, between the "romantic" and the absurd, and between the text and the illustration. He shows how

Lear's work demonstrates these characteristics. Tigges concentrates upon "The Dong with the Luminous Nose" and asks how the main characteristics of nonsense fit the poem. In his reply he shows how any suggestion of meaning or sense in the poem is simultaneously taken away so that the poem ultimately creates its own reality. The poem, therefore, demonstrates another important characteristic, and that is that nonsense assumes the world is "autonomous." Nonsense, therefore, creates its own reality with language; it does not imitate reality (257). Within the book Tigges offers what he calls a "new" definition of nonsense. Even though it is by no means a definitive one, perhaps it is appropriate to give his attempt.

> It is a narrative genre in which the seeming presence of one or more "sensible" meanings is kept in balance by a simultaneous absence of such a meaning. This balance is established by the absence of emotionally laden connotations and associations and by a creative play with the rules of language, logic and form. (255–56)

Critics, of course, continue to try and describe nonsense's seemingly amorphous form. The most recent study of nonsense is Alison Rieke's *The Senses of Nonsense* (1992) in which Rieke returns to and examines the traditional opposition between sense and nonsense. Her study focuses on twentieth-century writers, but it takes some of its cues from Lear's limericks, stories, and verses. In her chapters on James Joyce, Gertrude Stein, Wallace Stevens, and Louis Zukofsky, Rieke develops the idea that these authors' various experimental and disruptive uses of language are not so much a denial of sense as they are an acceptance of it. Sense becomes a tool which writers manipulate, invert, and twist to create their nonsense. As Rieke's book proves, Lear continues to be an important figure in discussions about theories of nonsense. In a certain respect, he is still "the father of nonsense."

3: Lear: the Artist and Musician

> *It seems to me that in converting memories into tangible facts, — recollections & past time as it were into pictures, — lies the chief use & charm of a painter's life (I'm sure if it isn't, I don't know where it is, for technical study & manipulation will always be a bore to me.)*
>
> (*Later Letters of Edward Lear*, 189)

FROM THE TIME HE was a very young man, Lear earned his living as an illustrator and painter. At first he worked as an illustrator, primarily of birds and animals. So skilful was he that his drawings and prints caught the attention of established figures like John Gould and Sir William Jardine. The result was that in his twenties Lear contributed to numerous natural history volumes. Among these are *A Century of Birds from the Himalayan Mountains* (1834), *Illustrations of British Ornithology*, vols. 3 and 4 (1834), *A Monograph of the Ramphastidae, or Family of Toucans* (1834), *A History of Quadrupeds, including the Cetacea* (1837), and *The Birds of Europe* (1832-1837). People were especially impressed by a volume of hand-colored lithographs, *The Family of Psittacidae or Parrots* (1830-1832) that Lear produced and had privately printed before he was twenty-years old. His brilliant use of color, the sharpness of his lines, the iridescence of the birds' plumage, and, most of all, his sense of a particular parrot's posture and idiosyncracies give his studies, in Susan Hyman's words, "an uncanny physical appearance" (26). The birds stare back at the viewer as if discovered in the midst of a previously unrecorded moment. Those who saw his prints thought them more than equal to Audubon's. Indeed, if Lear had continued to work exclusively as a natural history illustrator, he would probably now be better known than Audubon. Perhaps one of the best tributes to his abilities is the fact that birds have been named after him. Vivien Noakes, in the catalogue of the 1985 Royal Academy Exhibit lists them. They are the *Anodorhynchus leari* (Lear's Macaw), *Lopochroa Leari* (Lear's Cockatoo), and *Pyrrhulopsis tabuensis* (Tabuan Parrot) (209–10).

Around the age of twenty-five Lear, however, decided to change course and to travel and become a landscape painter. Although there were initially occasions when he still produced a few natural history drawings, Lear now devoted his attention to his painting. For the rest of his life he sketched, painted thousands of watercolors, labored over his large oil paintings, prepared his watercolor sketches for his travel books, and in the later years worked diligently on his illustrations for Tennyson's poems. By the time he died, Lear had produced over thirty thousand sketches and paintings. (The Houghton Library at Harvard University, alone, has a collection of nearly thirty–five hundred sketches and watercolors.)

Lear often worked from the early hours in the morning to the time darkness fell. He earned his living painting for patrons and selling his work that he exhibited in rooms where he traveled. Sometimes Lear found this mode of selling mildly pleasing. For instance, in a letter to Emily Tennyson (March 6, 1861), he writes about showing his paintings in his London rooms. The visitors came

> sometimes 20 at a time — of all kinds of phases of life: sometimes — for 3 hours no one comes: — so then I partly sleep, & partly draw pages of a new Nonsense book. If I sleep, I wake up savagely at some new comer's entrance, & they go away abashed. If I write nonsense, I am pervaded with smiles, & please the visitors. (As quoted in Noakes, 180)

About ten years later, in Cannes, Lear shows less patience with his need to exhibit his work and deal with his potential customers. In a letter to William Holman Hunt, the Pre-Raphaelite painter, he grumbles:

> for beauty of scenery, Cannes seemed the properest spot — but I, who have tried it for 3 years, judged otherwise. The first year I was there, there also happened to be many of my friends — & so I sold a good many drawings: — but afterwards, the true character of the place became evident, — a haunt of rich or Aristocratic people — all perhaps good — but all <u>absolutely</u> idle. All smiles & goodness if they could take up the whole of an artist's time — "we shall be so delighted if you will let us come & sit in your studio while you work!" — said one of many gt. ladies to me — "we will stay all the day! we should never be tired!" — but on the Artist showing a little notion of independence & self assertion — he was quite thrown by, & other

painters — awful daubers! — taken up — or art altogether ignored. (As quoted in Noakes, 253)

When Lear was not exhibiting his work, he was traveling extensively throughout Europe and the middle East and eventually to India sketching and painting places both familiar and unfamiliar to his public. At other times he busily and nervously prepared canvases for the Royal Academy exhibitions and hoped for good reviews and profitable sales. Occasionally he worried about his lack of formal training, so between 1849 and 1852 he set aside time to take lessons at the Royal Academy Schools and to paint under the tutelage of William Holman Hunt so that he might improve his techniques as an oil painter and feel more confident. Under the influence of Hunt, Lear tried to conform to the Pre-Raphaelite practice of painting on the spot and depicting the subject as accurately as possible. Lear's account of his trying to find sheep to put in the foreground of his Windsor Castle painting is worth reproducing, for it shows both how earnest he was and how detached he could be — enough to realize the absurdity of his efforts. The painting and the nonsense were never far away from one another. Lear writes:

> In order to make the foreground as good as I could, I have been trying all sorts of ways to paint sheep of a good size. First, I went to a friend the Rectory of Gt. Berkhamsted — but his sheep were so wild I could do nothing, & being caught, made so great a noise that my friend became nervous, & I was obliged to go away, lest he should preach from Samuel's question about the bleating of the sheep in his ears.
>
> Then I went to Hastings, but though I made many small drawings, I could not find good South Down Sheep near enough, or otherwise available to be painted large on so large a canvas.
>
> Lastly, I came here: — but the infinite obstacles owing to the size of the picture, the sheering of the sheep, the growth of the lambs &tc &tc &tc &tc &tc &tc, have at last worn me out utterly, therefore I shall give up all idea of doing the sheep as <u>large</u> as I intended, & confine myself to a simple foreground of green, with distant sheep .... (Edward Lear to Lord Derby, June 15, 1853. As quoted in Noakes, 116–17)

This diligence stayed with Lear so that when he eventually found the time to begin his project to illustrate Tennyson's poems, he worked ceaselessly, especially in his last years.

The Criticism

The responses to Lear's natural history illustrations have been, with a few exceptions, enthusiastic; the reactions to his paintings, however, have, on the whole, been less forthcoming. Critics have argued over the merits of his watercolors and his oils. Many have proposed that his watercolors, although not always equal to the masterpieces of nineteenth-century landscape painting, are superior to the oils, for unlike the oils, they are spontaneous, lively, and more "poetical." A few critics, however, have preferred the oils and have found them also to be "poetic." Most have admired the paintings for their accuracy but have faulted them for their lack of originality. The consensus tends to be that Lear was a conservative, yet accomplished, artist who would have received far more recognition if he had been more discriminating. Critics point out that Lear, so eager for sales and patrons, exhibited his work too readily and displayed the bad with the good. More recently, though, critics such as Jeremy Maas have acknowledged that Lear was "one of the most original landscape painters in the nineteenth century" (*Victorian Painters*, 100), and many now think more highly of his grand oil paintings than previously.

Unlike his commitment to his illustrating and painting, Lear's involvement with music was occasional or incidental. Although he was not formally trained, Lear often composed settings for poems and entertained his friends, sometimes for two or three hours, by playing and singing them. He apparently could not read music, so when there was interest in publishing a few of his songs, others had to transcribe them for him. The handful of critics who have written about his music recognize both its charm and its amateurism.

The Natural History Illustrations

Lear's natural history drawings and prints have almost universally elicited favorable responses. Immediately after he produced — at the age of twenty-three — the first part of his *Illustrations of the Family of Psittacidae, or Parrots* (1830), N. A. Vigors, Edward T. Bennett, and Thomas Bell proposed that Lear become an associate of the prestigious Linnean (also, Linnaean) Society. Many other contemporaries were quick with words of praise. Sir William Jardine, for instance, spoke of Lear's "beautiful and interesting illustrations," and William Swainson, the zoologist who was also a lithographer and student of Audubon, after seeing a copy of part 9 of the *Psittacidae* wrote enthusiastically about Lear's "beautiful work." In his letter to Lear, Swainson exclaims that the print of the red and yellow macaw is

> equal to any figure ever painted by Barraband or Audubon, for grace of design, perspective, or anatomical accuracy. I am so particularly pleased with these, that I should feel much gratified by possessing a

duplicate copy of each [the New Holland Palaeornis and the red and yellow macaw]. They will then be framed, as fit companions in my drawing-room to hang by the side of a pair by my friend Audubon. (As quoted in Reade, 9)

Lear's work soon caught the attention of other illustrators and producers of natural history books. He was able to earn modest commissions by supplying drawings and illustrations of birds and animals for over twenty-three natural history volumes, one of which was the privately printed *Gleanings from the Menagerie and Aviary at Knowsley Hall* (1846). Most of the volumes to which he contributed appeared in the 1830s and 1840s. In his lifetime Lear also received indirect praise from those who copied his work. One of these, Bourjot Saint-Hilaire, "borrowed" six of Lear's bird plates for his *Histoire Naturelle des Perroquets* (1837). Perhaps the only mild exception to the contemporary critics' unanimous praise occurs in the preface by Dr. John Edward Gray of the British Museum to the *Gleanings*, where he writes that "the chief value [of Lear's illustrations] consists in their being accurate representations of living specimens." Although Gray fails to remark on the plates' aesthetic qualities, his remarks are not inappropriate — he was, after all, a scientist interested in accurate representations. He himself had produced such books as *Illustrations of Indian Zoology*.

After Lear's death this high regard for the natural history studies never declined — although, as with his art painting, there were moments when the nonsense writing so overwhelmed everything else that the public paid little or no heed to these studies.

In the twentieth century, studies tracing the history of bird books give Lear's work a prominent place. For instance, Sir Sacheverell Sitwell in his *Fine Bird Books: 1700-1900* (1953) speaks of Lear as "perhaps the best of all bird painters," and C. E. Jackson in *Bird Illustrators: Some Artists in Early Lithography* (1975) comments upon the "scientific accuracy" (35) of Lear's work and suggests that because of this close, exacting labor, his eyes grew weak and he could no longer continue. Jackson's evaluation of Lear's work is interesting and worth repeating, for it differs slightly from others' in that Jackson is not quite as ready as most to offer unqualified praise. He is, however, eager to point out that Lear is a "pioneer" in lithography. He writes:

> Lear's birds are fascinating insofar as they have decided personalities of their own, sometimes almost whimsical characters. He combined accuracy of portrayal with artistically pleasing design. His birds are not full of life and animation, but neither are they stuffed specimens. His best pictures are those drawn from live models. He stands on the borderline between the stiff portraits of the metal engravers and the

freer, softer figures of the lithographers. Much of his work is in the detailed, fine-lined style of the engravers, but his figures are often shown in motion — either moving their heads or walking. His backgrounds are poor — a curious fact considering he was to spend the rest of his life as a landscape painter, but apart from Audubon no other bird-artist of the time was producing full habitat scenes and landscapes for their bird figures. He pointed the way to a freer, livelier depiction of birds by the lithographic method, which was taken a step further by Gould. Indeed, Gould learnt much from Lear, and profited financially, whereas Lear the pioneer, had never been sufficiently rewarded. (37–38)

Perhaps the only critic in the twentieth century to take Lear's natural history prints less seriously than other critics is Jeremy Mass who in *Victorian Painters* (1969) dismisses them by suggesting that they "belong more to literature than to art," and by concluding that they "are little more than an agreeable footnote to nineteenth century painting" (84).

In a more recent study of bird illustrations, the 1988 catalogue accompanying the exhibition entitled "The Bird Illustrated: 1500-1900" held at the New York Public Library, Roger Tory Peterson remarks that Lear "might have become the brightest star in the galaxy of bird illustrators had he not turned to landscape painting in his twenties" (8). Philip Hofer's remark eight years earlier that Lear was "perhaps the greatest draughtsman of birds in European culture" (Hyman, 9) seems less inflated in this context.

The first of the major studies of Lear's natural history work was written by Brian Reade, formerly Keeper of Prints and Drawings at the Victoria and Albert Museum. In 1949 he published a lengthy essay entitled *Edward Lear's Parrots*. In 1978 the monograph was reissued under the title *An Essay on Edward Lear's Illustrations of the Family of Psittacidae or Parrots*. (In 1947 Reade had also written a short article on "The Birds of Edward Lear" for *Signature*.) This monograph still stands as one of the most informed pieces about Lear's bird and animal illustrations. Reade offers the reader a biographical background and follows Lear's career as a natural history artist. Among other things he points out that even as a child or adolescent Lear displayed "an ardent love for birds and animals" (6) and that later in his life Lear, seeking to escape the "humiliation" of his epilepsy, found reassurance and comfort in this love. He also remarks that if Lear had received traditional schooling rather than the informal tutoring given him by his sisters Ann and Sarah, "the Lear familiar to us might never have emerged" (6). After supplying names, dates, and details about Lear's working relationships with some of the leading naturalists of his time, Reade emphasizes Lear's uniqueness in working from living models — an exception to those who worked from stuffed models in studios — and his art of depicting his parrots from "casual points of view." He notices how Lear arrests the animals and birds "in the arcs of complex movements so their shapes are revealed as never before, except perhaps in certain Dutch paintings of the late seventeenth century" (7). Reade, however, informs his readers that Lear was not the first to work from live models. Although Lear never mentions knowing William Harvey, it was he who set the precedent of working from live specimens and broke away from "the formal side-view representation of his subjects" (7).

In his monograph Reade also describes the lithographic process and explains that Lear's "choice of the lithographic medium for the *Psittacidae* was due in some degree to the circumstances of his education" — he had no apprenticeship in engraving or etching (10). It was a choice, according to Reade, which allowed him to close the distance between the drawing and the print, and which allowed him to develop into "one of the soundest of craftsmen among early lithographers" (10).

Just as his contemporaries compared Lear to Audubon, so does Reade who suggests that Audubon "never arrived at Lear's romantic and intuitive comprehension of the movements of birds and the articulation of their feathered forms" (10).

At the end of his essay, Reade comments upon the relationship between the natural history illustrations and the nonsense drawings. His remarks are interesting:

> it remains only to be pointed out, what has so far been ignored, that the illustrations to the written Nonsenses are often the cliches of a skilled draughtsman, not much interested in human figures as such, but with considerable experience in drawing birds and animals — birds especially. (14)

In the preface to the 1978 edition, the editor, Gavin Bridson, Librarian of the Linnean Society, gives a publishing history of the *Psittacidae* and an account of Lear's association with the Linnean Society.

The second major publication also concentrates on Lear's ornithological prints. Susan Hyman's *Edward Lear's Birds* (1980) follows Reade's lead but goes further by presenting more particulars and reproducing full-page illustrations from the many volumes to which he contributed. Hyman includes some animal illustrations. The book's small folio size does justice to Lear's pictures and gives the reader a good sense of them in the original. The full-size reproductions of the "Spectacled Owl," the "Marsh Harrier," and the "Great Auk," for instance, are especially striking.

Hyman identifies four reasons why Lear's *Psittacidae* sets new standards in ornithological publishing: he was the first to choose the large folio size; the first to work from living example (a claim that Reade, as we have seen, qualifies by pointing out that there was a precedent for this practice); the first to produce his own lithographs; and the first to devote an entire book to one family of birds. In more detail than in Reade's study, Hyman's describes Lear's methods of illustrating and printing and gives a publishing history of his contributions to the various natural history books. Hyman writes at more length about his relationships with such individuals as Lord Derby and the Goulds and offers a more complete sense of the cultural context in which Lear was producing his illustrations. Like Reade, she is sensitive to Lear's endowing his birds "with some measure of his own whimsy and intelligence" (45) and his drawing on his scientific studies to create his nonsense (76). As a result, throughout her book Hyman scatters Lear's nonsense drawings of birds as if to reveal what the natural history prints merely half suggest. The nonsense drawings make explicit the personalities that lie just beneath the surface of his more formal natural history pictures.

Hyman also writes briefly on Lear's landscape paintings and his Tennyson illustrations. She joins the many when she suggests that "the inspiration with which he sketched both animals and landscapes was never present in his huge exhibition pieces" (73). And like others she also addresses the question of why, in his twenties, he chose to leave such a successful career as a natural history illustrator and take up landscape painting. Hyman suggests that his enjoying the sketching tours he went on as a young man, his longing for independence, his desire to travel, his health, and his eyesight which was "too weak for the minutiae of animal studies" all played a part. She concludes the book with a helpful bibliography listing all the natural history volumes to which he contributed. It is interesting to note that when Hyman compares Lear's and Audubon's prints, she finds Lear's lacking "Audubon's theatricality and atmosphere." She also suggests that Lear's prints "endure as portraits of individuals rather than species" (28) — a nice point.

Between the major publications are a number of short articles in which reviewers and critics build upon or reiterate Reade's monograph: Adrian Bury's "The Other Side of Edward Lear" (1963), Maureen Lambourne's "Birds of a Feather: Edward Lear and Elizabeth Gould" (1964), Christopher Neve's "There was a Young Person of ... Edward Lear's Parrots" (1973), and Colin J. Bailey's "Edward Lear at Knowsley" (1975). There were also exhibitions which included the illustrations. The most significant of these was in March 1975 at the Walker Art Gallery, Liverpool (close to Knowsley Hall). The gallery showed forty of Lear's zoological drawings. In reviewing the exhibit, Colin Bailey writing for *Apollo* states that the drawings "revealed unequivocally qualities in Lear's draughtsmanship, such as his highly developed feeling for decoration and design" (394).

Since the publication of Susan Hyman's book in 1980 there have been other articles on Lear's natural history illustrations. In"The Runcible Life and Works of the Remarkable Edward Lear" (1981) John Kastner speaks of Lear as the "best natural-history artist England has ever produced" (107–8). He points out how "ornithologically correct" the drawings are and reminds the readers that Lear's "meticulous yet lifelike birds were ranked with Audubon's" (109). Other articles like Maureen Lambourne's "Edward Lear and John Gould" (1984) and Vivien Noakes's "The Sense and Nonsense of Edward Lear" (1985) also continue to convey admiration for Lear's work and especially to laud his capabilities as a draftsman. There is one recent article, though, which is less than enthusiastic about the natural history illustrations. In "How Pleasant Is It to Know Mr. Lear?" (1986), Michael Patrick Hearn writes that although the prints for *The Family of Psittacidae or Parrots* are "lovely, both highly finished and gorgeously colored," they are, in his opinion, too "scientific" and, therefore, "generally lifeless." His is one of the few dissenting voices in a century of praise.

Exhibitions in the 1980s have helped enhance Lear's stature as a natural history illustrator. The important 1985 exhibit at the Royal Academy of Arts in London that traveled to the National Academy of Design in New York gave considerable space to Lear's bird and animal paintings, drawings, and prints. Their presence among the rest of Lear's work invited the public not only to understand Lear's versatility but also to see how one part of his work interacts with another — how, for instance, his natural history illustrations become the materials for his nonsense drawings and limericks. Another important show was the 1988 exhibition entitled "Edward Lear's Birds" which was mounted in honor of Lear's centenary at the Ruskin Gallery.

In terms of interpretive critical work there has been little. Most recently *Victorian Poetry* (1992) has published an article by Ann C. Colley entitled "Edward Lear's Anti-Colonial Bestiary." In her essay Colley discusses the disparity between the words of the limericks and the drawings that accompany them. She suggests that one reason why there are differences between them is that the drawings, unlike the verses, are "political." They reveal a Lear who is sensitive to the fact that animals are being used as emblems of England's dominion over remote territories and nations. In particular, they show his impatience with the practice of "colonizing" the animal world. To illustrate her point Colley discusses, in detail, Lear's career as a natural history illustrator, a profession that put him in touch with bird and animal collectors, zoologists, keepers, hunters, and breeders. She then focuses on how Lear uses his nonsense drawings to achieve a kind of revenge, on the animals' behalf, against those who attempted to manage, organize, cage, domesticate, and dominate their captives. She concludes that through his natural history drawings of animals and birds in which his subjects stare back at the person regarding them and through his nonsense depictions of animals and birds gaining the upper hand over humans, Lear slyly rebelled against the practice of using these "beasts" as commodities and icons of imperialism. The article derives from Colley's reading of Harriet Ritvo's *The Animal Estate* (1987), a book which examines the relationship of people and animals in nineteenth-century Britain.

The Paintings

It is, perhaps, only recently that Lear's paintings have received the full attention they merit or that Lear desired. Although his contemporaries were well aware of his profession as a painter and although patrons bought his watercolors and oils, the popularity of his nonsense verses has tended to make these accomplishments insignificant by comparison. As Vivien Noakes points out in her recent and comprehensive study of Lear's art (*The Painter Edward Lear*, 1991), people undervalued the worth of his paintings until 1929 when in February and March many of his travel watercolors and drawings that he had left to Franklin Lushington came on the market and caught the critics' attention. (There were auction sales at Hodgson's and Sotheby's). A few months later part of Lord Northbrook's collection also came on the market. Before these events his reputation as an artist was in such decline that it was possible to purchase his large oil paintings for a few pounds. One sold for as little as twelve pounds two shillings. Since 1929, though, Lear's standing as a painter has steadily increased so that now, according to Noakes, one of the large oils can demand at least one-quarter of a million pounds — quite a difference from the time the poet William Plomer, according to John Lehmann, became an enthusiast for Lear's paintings and drawings and picked up "examples ... in various print shops in and around London ... for a few shillings, or at the most a pound or two" (92).

The criticism of Lear's art work has followed a similar pattern. As the years have passed, more and more critics have chosen to write about his paintings and have found them to be of value. What follows, then, is not so much a discussion of what his art accomplishes but rather a chronological narrative of the increasing attention paid to his work and of the various ways in which people have discussed its strengths and weaknesses.

The Nineteenth and Early Twentieth Centuries

Even though Lear's nonsense captured most of the public's attention, his art never entirely disappeared from view. Early reviews of his nonsense books, for instance, rarely failed to mention that he was a landscape artist. There were also contemporary reviews of some of his paintings, especially those larger oils that were selected for major exhibitions at the Royal Academy of Arts. Not all these responses were favorable, however. As an example, Noakes refers to Tom Taylor's June 11, 1860, commentary on *The Cedars of Lebanon* which dismisses the painting as mere topography, without "poetic feeling" (*The Times*).

It was with the public exhibitions of his watercolors rather than his oils that the art world and increasingly the public started to take Lear more seriously. (Lady Strachey's 1907 and 1911 editions of Lear's letters also contributed to a growing appreciation, for they include reproductions of a few of his watercolor sketches.) In 1912 there was the first posthumous exhibition of Lear's painting that gave many an opportunity to see "the travel watercolours in all their freshness" (Noakes, *The Painter Edward Lear*, 106).

This exhibition seems to have started a trend to regard the watercolors as being superior to the oils. Ian Malcolm in *The Pursuit of Leisure* (1929), for instance, praises the watercolors and suggests that if Lear had been more selective in his lifetime and had not exhibited the bad with the good, he might have earned the praise he deserves. In 1930 the watercolors caught the attention of Martin Hardie who in *Art Work* declares that Lear "is far greater as draughtsman and painter" (114) than has previously been admitted. He suggests that if more of Lear's work were on display rather than hidden in private collections, the watercolors would receive the attention they deserve. After a brief sketch of Lear's artistic career, Hardie describes his methods of painting and then places him within the tradition of the nineteenth-century water-colorists. In his opinion, Lear is not "in the highest class with Cozzens and Girtin, Cox and De Wint, but he is a respectably good painter," even though he lacks "any flight of poetry or imagination" (118).

One of the most sensitive essays to be written about Lear's painting is a short piece, "Appreciation of Lear as a Painter," that Henry Strachey, Lady Strachey's brother-in-law, composed for the 1907 edition of the correspondence. Strachey opens his essay with the statement: "The landscape painting of Edward Lear has never been popular either with artists or the larger public" (xxxvi). He then wonders why "fellow-painters" (Henry Strachey was himself an artist) have been "slow to appreciate Lear's work." One reason, he suggests, is that Lear has separated himself from the current mode of landscape painting that represents a place's "atmosphere" and records how the light plays over the scene. Strachey is, of course, thinking of Turner and the "great schools of France" that "painted the scene for the sake of the light that fell on it, and not the light as an incident in the landscape" (xxxvii). Lear, Strachey writes, does not seem to have any sympathy with these principles; he only is interested in topographical details. Strachey explains:

> If he painted the Roman Campagna every sinew in the plain was lovingly recorded, as was every arch of the aqueducts, and even the lumps of the fallen masonry in the foreground. One is sometimes

tempted to think that when Lear painted an olive-tree near at hand against the sky he counted the leaves. A traveller could almost plan his route over a pass from one of this artist's faithful realisations of mountains. (xxxvii–xxxviii)

Strachey continues by remarking that Lear rarely paints clouds. For him skies are merely background material.

Although Strachey believes that for the reasons stated above Lear never can rank beside "the great masters of landscape," he does admire the paintings. Lear, he believes, has a "true sense of beauty." His paintings, therefore, are valuable because they reflect Lear's sense of nature's beauty and because they record it "with individuality." Strachey also appreciates Lear's subtle sense of color and his delicate style. His paintings, he suggests, are "always dignified and sincere" (xl). Strachey does not want to be among those who consider the paintings valuable because they represent "exactly some piece of country" (xxxix). Frequently when critics have responded to Lear's paintings, his oils in particular, they have emphasized this characteristic. Many are fond of recounting the stories of people who could tell the geology of a country from the paintings or could use the paintings to illustrate certain historical events. For instance, Professor Grundy reproduced many of the scenes Lear painted in the neighborhood of Thermopylae to illustrate his history of the Great Persian War.

During the 1930s reproductions of Lear's work began appearing in magazines and journals. For instance, the *Journal of the Royal Institute of British Architects* (February 1932) reproduced "Parnassus," a watercolor presented by Mrs. F. M. Noel to the Institute. In July 1934 *Antiques* reproduced one of his landscapes done in Corfu. The writer in the magazine expresses some mild surprise that Lear had not only made bird prints but also had painted landscapes. The writer had seen the watercolors in exhibitions in New York and California (26). This transatlantic connection has always been an active one, especially since two American collectors, Philip Hofer and William B. Osgood Field, began buying Lear's watercolors and drawings during this period. In 1942 they deposited their collections in the Houghton Library, Harvard. Bertha Coolidge Slade's privately printed catalogue of the Field collection, *Edward Lear on My Shelves*, appeared in 1933.

Of all the expressions of attention critics and connoisseurs paid to Lear's paintings in the 1930s, none, perhaps, created a larger audience for the work than Angus Davidson's sensitive biography, *Edward Lear: Landscape Painter and Nonsense Poet* (1938). The fact that the phrase "Landscape Painter" precedes "Nonsense Poet" in the book's title reflects the emphasis Davidson places on Lear's paintings. In this biography Davidson acknowledges what others in the 1930s had already realized, that Lear's paintings have taken a long time to be recognized. He notices that even though there have been exhibitions of his watercolors which have been praised by the critics, the general public is not aware of them. Davidson hopes to fill the gap, for he believes that Lear should take his place within the "great tradition of nineteenth-century water-colour painting." Throughout the book it is these watercolors, rather than the oil paintings, that receive most of the attention.

In chapter 13 Davidson discusses at length "Lear as Painter and Poet." He remarks on Lear's gifts as a draftsman and champions the watercolors and drawings, especially the later work, for their consequent fluidity of line. Like others before and after him, he judges the watercolors and drawings to be far superior to the carefully worked oils that, in his opinion, fail to come to life and tend to reflect Lear's lack of intrinsic enjoyment in executing them. If an oil is good, it is because it resembles his watercolor drawings. The oils are, according to Davidson, "little more than exceedingly accurate and well-constructed illustrations of well-chosen views." Davidson continues, "that a painter should make his own personal interpretation of nature, should put something of his own feelings into his picture, did not occur to him" (182). The worst of the oils reveals the tightness and literalness imposed by the Pre-Raphaelite principles. Davidson does recognize, though, that "Lear could scarcely be called a true Pre-Raphaelite in his outlook." He explains:

> his affinities with Mantegna and Botticelli were highly questionable; but since the nature of his paintings was essentially literary and descriptive, there is no doubt that Hunt's technical advice, especially in matters of detail, was of great service to him in his oil-painting. Above all, it had restored his self-confidence. (85–86)

Davidson especially praises Lear's later work in which he is "most completely himself" and his lines are "supple" and "sweeping" (186). But echoing Ian Malcolm's earlier criticism, Davidson faults Lear for his absence of self-criticism and lack of discrimination of his own work which led him into exhibiting much that was not worth displaying.

In the same year, R. L. Mégroz wrote an article for *The Cornhill Magazine* that also praises the watercolors. Mégroz comments upon Lear's "devotion to clear and accurate detail" (178) and, interestingly enough, "his avoidance of suggestion or evanescence of impression, such as Turner ... would exploit" (178). He does, however, fault Lear for his inability to be bold or original, especially in the finished pieces. Like Davidson he believes it is only in the sketches that Lear becomes more truly creative and discovers the "ultimate freedom of individuality" (179).

The same year Davidson's biography and Mégroz's article appeared, The Fine Art Society (London) held an exhibition of Lear's more serious work as a topographical landscape painter. The combination of Davidson's biography, Mégroz's article, and this exhibition, naturally, did much to enhance Lear's reputation as an artist, and especially, as a watercolorist.

The 1940s and 1950s

In the 1940s there continued to be small exhibitions of Lear's art work. One was at the Redfern Gallery. A reviewer for *Apollo* (1942) remarks that the watercolors are "different from those of the British water-colourists" and for this reason Lear is "not so highly esteemed in his generation as he is to-day." He adds:

> He was in his day acclaimed mainly for the topographical vividness of his literary and pictorial "Journals". Now we see in his best water-colours a structural pithiness, a creative freedom which proclaims a pronounced individuality. (98)

The reviewer regards the exhibition as a "re-discovery."

The small exhibitions continued in the 1950s and so did the interest in Lear. (Davidson's biography of Lear was revised in the 1950s.) His oils, though, were still disparaged and did not fetch high prices. Noakes documents, for instance, that in 1954 the six-foot *Acropolis* was sold for fifteen guineas, and the seven-foot *Windsor Castle* fetched thirty guineas.

In 1958 the Arts Council (London) mounted an exhibition of Lear's work which did much to keep his name before the public and to inform them that Lear did more than compose nonsense verses. Brian Reade who introduced the Lear Exhibition informed his audience, for instance, about Lear's methods of sketching and painting. Reade explains:

> He would set out with his gear and his manservant, select a site, lift his spectacles, gaze at the scene before him through a monocular glass, and then, readjusting his spectacles, begin to draw rapidly in pencil. Certain details would be inscribed in longhand with colour notes in Lear's own special phonetic spelling, "rox" for rocks, "ski" for sky, and so on. Sometimes he would apply water-colour in generalized tints over large areas with great dash. Much of his work must have been done indoors. In the evening too he would "pen over" the pencil and water-colour sketches, graduating minutely the receding planes and outlining the forms rather sharply, so as to give an effect of crystalline elegance. (*Victorian Painters*, 100)

The reviews of the 1958 show at the Arts Council were favorable, but as usual the debate concerning the merits of the watercolors versus the oils continues.

For instance, although he enjoyed the exhibition, Horace Shipp, the reviewer for *Apollo* complained about the "unexpected emphasis on the oils" which Lear "hated so much" (48). Shipp prefers to think of Lear as a "born" artist who did not really care for art. He explains, "Lear was an artist who almost hated art; but as he was able to do it swiftly, and had a scientist's eye for structure and surface, he painstakingly devoted all his time to earning his living by creating and organising the sales of his pictures" (48). Another reviewer, G. S. Whittet, writing for *The Studio*, speaks more positively of the Arts Council show. For him it is one of the most amusing and "personal of any relating to an English artist." Whittet, however, is unusual, for he does not care for the topographical drawings that the others praise so highly. He finds them lacking in spontaneity. Contrary to the trend, Whittet prefers the "impressive" oil paintings. In them he finds "virtuosity" (125). The reviewer for *The Burlington Magazine* (1958), though, is less responsive to the oils. He speaks of them as being "mechanical and overworked," with "a pathetic misapplication of genuine artistic talent" (295). This reviewer, therefore, keeps the company of those who prefer the watercolors to the oils.

The 1960s and 1970s

In the 1960s Lear's paintings continued to be exhibited and discussed, reproduced, or mentioned in such magazines as *The Connoisseur, Apollo,* and *Country Life.*

In all the notices of exhibits, there is still the need either to explain to readers or to acknowledge that Lear, the nonsense writer, was also an artist. Reviewers note that his watercolors have recently "come into their own" — that they are in "vogue" and that one must "pay a good deal of money for them" (*The Connoisseur*, 1962). The reviewer in *The Connoisseur*, though, suggests that judging by the small oil *Mount Parnassus,* on view at the Fine Art Society, London, Lear "was an even better oil painter" than a watercolorist. A "deep poetic vein" runs through them (49). So the debate continues.

New and rediscovered work was also catching the art world's attention. For instance, in 1964 the public had a chance to see a loan exhibition of Lear's watercolors from Corfu.

In 1965 Lear's watercolors still received considerable attention, for they continued to be exhibited at the Annual Exhibition of Watercolours and Drawings; reproductions of Lear's watercolors are to be seen in magazines that are advertizing the shows. Paul Grinke in his review of the ninety-second exhibition for *Apollo* speaks of Lear as "an artist of exceptional merit" and praises the "distinctive fastidiousness and virtuosity" of his watercolors.

In the 1960's more of Lear's work was finding its way into the auction room. His paintings seem to have been in fashion and in demand. For instance, Frank Davis writing for *Country Life* (November 4, 1965) refers to the fact that Lear's "highly-accomplished" paintings of Italy, the Aegean, and the Levant are frequently seen in the auction rooms and that one of the less viewed scenes (of Ceylon) recently sold at Christie's for 420 guineas (1185).

One of the most significant critical events, though, of the 1960s was the publication of Philip Hofer's *Edward Lear as a Landscape Draughtsman* (1967). This book presents and discusses Lear's landscape drawings and watercolors, mainly those housed at Harvard University. (The book does not, however, deal with either the oils or the nonsense drawings.) In addition to reproducing 110 drawings, Hofer not only discusses the tradition of landscape drawing that Lear inherits, he also describes Lear's technical procedures, his development as a draftsman, and the relationship between his drawings and paintings. Hofer then speaks of the growing appreciation for Lear's landscape drawings and concludes by giving the reader a sense of the present status of the Harvard collection. Throughout Hofer is intent upon reminding his readers that Lear is "one of the leading British figures" (vii), who should not be overlooked, and he is intent upon appraising Lear's drawings so he might correct what he senses has either been misunderstood or overlooked. What is interesting about Hofer's appraisal, though, is not so much his praise of Lear's abilities as a topographer; nor his description of Lear's methods of working; nor his sense of the "intimate kinship" between what Lear saw and expressed; nor his gratitude to Lear for having, through his drawings, left a record of places that have now irrevocably changed. What is fascinating, rather, is Hofer's cataloguing of Lear's faults as an artist. Essentially he criticizes Lear for not being another Turner or a Constable and for failing to learn from the masters of the past. In his opinion because Lear did not study these masters of landscape painting seriously enough, his work, especially his finished pieces, tends to be stiff and lifeless. Furthermore, these overworked paintings get caught in the ruts of learned conventional practices. Echoing Henry Strachey's earlier criticism, Hofer writes that Lear seems to have neither the interest nor the ability to represent Turner's "turbulent seas" or Constable's "stormy clouds" (vi). Moreover, Hofer criticizes Lear for his "terrible tendency to insert more and more unnecessary detail" (55). This habit creates paintings that are more "deadly serious" than alive (56). The reviews in the *Contemporary Review* and *Apollo* of Hofer's book reflect his sense that Lear is a traditionalist and a conservative artist who once finding his style sticks to it. The same year as *Edward Lear as Landscape Draughtsman* came out, The Worcester Art Museum held what Hofer called "the first important exhibition in America of Edward Lear's original work." In the catalogue, *Edward Lear: Painter, Poet and Draughtsman* (1968), Hofer reiterates his conviction that Lear "was not a great painter, but he was a very fine topographical draughtsman." This exhibition also was seen in London at Gordon and Fox.

Vivien Noakes's biography, *Edward Lear: The Life of a Wanderer* (1968), also contributed significantly to the growing appreciation of Lear's paintings, but like Hofer's study, it too includes some negative criticism. Noakes devotes many pages to documenting, in detail, Lear's career as a landscape painter and his attempts to learn more about his art and give himself more confidence by entering the Royal Academy and by putting himself under William Holman Hunt's tutelage. In one chapter on the subject, she remarks that the watercolors are "enjoying a reputation they never had" in Lear's lifetime (174). She then continues:

> One reason for this, one amongst several, is that Lear let himself be patronized. The trouble, of course, was that he simply could not afford to upset anyone who was thinking of buying his work, but the result was that though many of the people who had his paintings derived a great deal of pleasure from them, few felt that they had bought anything of value. (174)

To help prove her point, Noakes quotes a letter from Lady Waldegrave to Lear in which she offers a doubtful or qualified praise of a few paintings she has purchased from him. She writes, "I fell in love at first sight with your beautiful pictures. They far and far surpass my expectations and I am miserable at not knowing where I can find a good place for them" (176–77).

The rest of Noakes's criticism echoes what other reviewers have also complained of: that Lear exhibited the good with the bad — he did not have the power or the desire to discriminate between the superior and the inferior pieces; and that he never fully understood what he was doing when he painted his large oils. He had hoped they would bring him fame (and money), but the problem was that he did not master the medium. Noakes comments on the fact that Lear thought these oils, rather than his watercolors, were his real achievement.

Because Lear was now becoming more of an established figure in the art world, Jeremy Maas in his comprehensive study of Victorian art (*Victorian Painters*, 1969) speaks at length about Lear. Significantly, in his discussion he tends to favor the watercolors (he does, though, reproduce one of the oils). He writes, "No artist understood the geological characteristics of strange wild landscape so well ..." (99). At the same time, though, Maas is sensitive to the romantic elements in Lear's rendition of landscape. In a paragraph he offers his critical appraisal:

> Lear's painting was always inspired by the romantic element in landscape. Jagged mountains, huge trees, distant views at sunset, precipices, ravines: these he treated with technical skill and a character

absolutely unique to him. The structure of his watercolours is predominately linear, and in his oil paintings his handling of paint is at times almost abstract: an oil sketch by Lear can resemble the work of Sidney Nolan. A Pre-Raphaelite influence, by reason of his association with Holman Hunt in the 'fifties, is also discernible: the mountainous background of *The Scapegoat* looks as though it might have been painted by Lear. (100)

Lear's work continued to be on display in the 1970s. One of the most significant was a loan exhibit from the Gennadius Library in Athens (1971-1972) — the Library, according to John Lehmann, had acquired an assortment of Lear's Greek watercolors in 1929 for £25. Writing in 1977 Lehmann remarks, "There were 192 separate items; they could scarcely be worth less than £25,000 at today's prices" (92). In the introduction to the catalogue, *Edward Lear in Greece*, Philip Hofer renews the praise he had expressed in his 1967 book and speaks of Lear's drawings of Greece as being "the best artistic interpretations that exist before modern construction, tourism, and industrialization visibly intruded, spoiling the calm nostalgic beauty of the Greek mainland, and the islands, both in the Aegean and Ionian Seas" (7). The drawings record a landscape that is no longer available.

Lear's paintings were gaining more of a solid reputation and, therefore, commanded more space in such magazines as *The Connoisseur*. For instance, Edward Morris's 1971 article on "The Beausire Collection of Watercolours" devotes a number of paragraphs to Lear's sketches. In the article Morris recalls the fact that Lear took lessons from William Holman Hunt and wonders why Lear did not stick to Hunt's advice to paint the final version "on the spot." Morris is impatient with the quantity of notes Lear wrote on his sketches. He finds, though, a similarity between Hunt's and Lear's choice of colors. Morris also links Lear's work to the eighteenth-century linear tradition.

John Lehmann's *Edward Lear and his World* (1977) also gives considerable space to Lear's landscape painting. He points out that Lear "was one of a large company of English artists of his time dedicated to their profession as 'topographical painters.'" Lehmann goes on to say that Lear was "not the greatest of them" but that he was modern, for he "had an altogether exceptional gift for bold simplification of line — a gift that comes out equally strongly in his nonsense drawings — and for creating mood by the simplest means" (95–96). Unlike those who find little or nothing of Turner's influence, Lehmann discovers "Turneresque" moments in the maturer pieces. He also comments upon the paintings' fidelity to accurate detail. To make his point, he quotes Sir Osbert Lancaster who writes:

the careful recording vision that had made him so superlative an illustrator of natural history books, allied with that rapid calligraphic execution which gives to his comic drawings their eternal freshness, renders the best of his sketches records of the Greek countryside which have never been surpassed. (97)

The 1980s and on

The public's awareness of Lear as a painter increased notably in the 1980s. A number of books and articles appeared. Ina Rae Hark's study of Lear for the Twayne Series, for instance, discusses the paintings, even though her emphasis is on the "nonsenses." She agrees with those critics who wished Lear had been more discriminating and with those, like Noakes, who speak of his pragmatism — his practice of "cranking out" pictures to sell. She also joins those who find his watercolor sketches superior to his large oil paintings. To support her point, she quotes Noakes's opinion on the subject:

He never fully understood what he was doing when he painted in oils, and in his anxiety he often overworked the pictures until all the sparkle had gone and the fluid, rhythmical movement which made the watercolors so delightful had been ground to a standstill. (11)

Although the section on the paintings in Hark's book is helpful, it offers no new material. Several other books that were published in the 1980s, however, do bring materials otherwise not always available before the reading public. These books are a facsimile edition of Lear's *Views in the Seven Ionian Islands* (with twenty tinted lithographic plates) (1986), Ruth Pitman's *Edward Lear's Tennyson* (1988), Philip Sherrard's *Edward Lear: The Corfu Years: A Chronicle Presented through his Letters and Journals* (1988), and Vidya Dehejia's *Impossible Picturesqueness: Edward Lear's Indian Watercolours, 1873-1875* (1989). All these books include a generous number of color and black and white reproductions.

Pitman's book, for instance, reproduces many drawings most people have not had the opportunity to see. She opens her book by summarizing the biographical materials already available but then goes on to discuss, in detail, the drawings Lear rendered and assembled to accompany Tennyson's poems. In her remarks she explains that Lear's illustrations are not literal representations of Tennyson's verses but rather capture the emotional suggestion of an individual line or verse. Using his large stock of travel drawings and paintings done over a lengthy period of time, Lear selected and worked over and copied those that related to the poems. Pitman makes several interesting remarks: that these drawings were never part of the work he did for a commission (an unusual circumstance since Lear worked so hard to sell his paintings and gain commissions); that they are essentially a history of Lear's own artistic past — they are "a record of his own artistic endeavour" (22); and that they are as much a summary of his own life experiences as they are a response to Tennyson's words. In detail, Pitman explains the stages through which the illustrations passed and offers a commentary upon each of the illustrations and its relationship to the poem it accompanies. Unlike Hofer, Pitman believes that Lear did feel the influence of Turner. She does, however, agree with those critics who find the sketches more satisfying to the eye than the meticulously completed pieces. Pitman suggests that Lear's sketches "often achieve an imaginative unity, a vitality which eludes the artist in his carefully finished" watercolors and oils (21).

Philip Sherrard's *Edward Lear: The Corfu Years: A Chronicle Presented through his Letters and Journals* (1989) has many color reproductions of paintings that are rarely displayed. It is full of color plates of paintings done while Lear was in residence in Corfu. These reproductions are beautifully printed and, consequently, give the reader a good sense of the originals. In an appended essay, entitled "Lear as a Landscape Painter," Sherrard agrees with the majority that Lear's most ambitious paintings, his large oils, are "by and large academic and lifeless" (234). They are so, he explains, because Lear chose to work within "neo-classical conventions." Sherrard, like so many others, prefers the watercolor drawings. They are superior, he explains, because they break away from these conventions — the "neo-classical fetters" (234) that bind the oil paintings — and reveal a subtlety of rhythm, line, and color. For Sherrard, these sketches engage the imagination; they are musical (234-35).

With the publication of *Impossible Picturesqueness: Edward Lear's Indian Watercolours, 1873-1875* (1989), readers were given yet another opportunity to glimpse at even more of Lear's paintings than they usually have a chance to view. In the introduction, the editor, Vidya Dehejia, writes about Lear's travels in India and his activity as an artist. Dehejia informs the reader that Lear produced more than two thousand Indian drawings (now housed at Harvard University), describes the "categories" or kinds of drawings he produced ("scraps," large watercolors, and finished oils and watercolors that Lear sold), and explains that many are covered with notations so that Lear could finish the sketch as accurately as possible. Dehejia also points out that sometimes Lear used photographs as an aid to drawing, "particularly when recording architectural structures that were exotic and unfamiliar." Lear, he remarks, seems to have purchased photographs "as aides-mémoire, to which he could refer when he completed his watercolours, perhaps several years later" (xiv).

Appended to *Impossible Picturesqueness* is an essay, "The Painter of Topographical Poetry," by Allen Staley. Staley places Lear's paintings within the "topographical" tradition — a genre of painting many, including Henry Fuseli, consider inferior because its purpose is purely to "provide information about the places shown" (109). Staley explains that Lear's traveling was not, of course, unusual; it was what many British artists did in order to produce topographical illustrations for books. He then speaks of Lear's possible indebtedness to such artists as Frederic Church and Turner. These two are "the paramount" influences on Lear's art "as it evolved away from the more-or-less standardised views of his early career" (110). All the same, Staley reminds the reader, Lear was "deeply conservative, becoming, if anything, increasingly old-fashioned as time passed" (111). However, Staley concludes, "Behind each choice of subject, each drawn line, each wash of colour, we can feel the personal stamp of the amiable eccentric, and intelligent observer of a wondrous exotic land" (112).

At the end of his essay, Staley touches upon the question of the relationship between Lear's paintings and his nonsense. It is this question that Ann C. Colley addresses in "Edward Lear's Limericks and the Reversals of Nonsense" (*Victorian Poetry,* 1988). Colley sees the limericks as reversals of the paintings.

Of all the publications in the 1980s, though, none did more to enhance Lear's reputation and to broaden the public's understanding of his life as an artist than the catalogue accompanying the 1985 Lear exhibit at the Royal Academy of Arts in London and at the National Academy of Design in New York. Like the exhibit it describes, the catalogue (*Edward Lear 1812-1888*) offers a sampling of Lear's varied talents and experiences. Furthermore, it, once and for all, lets people know that Lear was not primarily a nonsense writer. In her introduction to the catalogue, the editor, Vivien Noakes, emphasizes his work and life as a painter. Within the catalogue are many color reproductions of his work. Beneath each, Noakes comments upon the circumstances under which he composed and sold the particular piece. Noakes also offers such details as the size, medium, date, and location of the painting or print.

The essays within the catalogue also discuss his profession as a painter. Steven Runciman's essay, "Edward Lear," for instance, speaks of Lear as "a superb draughtsman" who was "never very good at the human figure" (16-17). He agrees with those who find the large oil paintings "over-finished," and those, like Hofer, who believe that his paintings are primarily valuable for their accuracy, their "historical evidence" — for their depictions of places that have been altered or destroyed. Another essay in the catalogue is Jeremy Maas's "From the Sublime to the Ridiculous: Edward Lear in his Artistic Context." Maas devotes his entire essay to Lear's sensitivity to the works of his artistic contemporaries and to the tradition of landscape painting. Maas refers, for example, to minor painters like Thomas Creswick, to the classical landscape tradition of Salvator Rosa and Claude Lorrain, to the teachings of John Ruskin, and to the works of Frederic Church and Turner. Referring to Ruskin, Maas writes:

> As a Victorian landscape painter, Lear could not have failed to respond to the teachings of Ruskin, whom he admired. He dutifully digested *Modern Painters*: thereafter his foregrounds came to acquire a concern for more carefully rendered detail, while the middle distances and backgrounds reflected the enthusiasm of both for the revelation of the great truths in nature implicit in the grander works of Turner. Lear had, however, already shown a gift for scientific accuracy in his early ornithological illustration: Ruskin's advocacy could be said, therefore, to have been anticipated by him at an early age. (19)

Following Maas's essay is a five-page section entitled "Lear on Art" which is a series of quotations from Lear on such figures as Titian, Turner, Church, and Hunt; on such institutions as the Royal Academy of Arts; and on such subjects as nature and the pleasures of painting. Throughout the catalogue Noakes provides a helpful and extensive commentary on each item displayed in the exhibit. These paragraphs contain valuable information about the circumstances under which individual paintings and sketches developed, and about their history.

The 1985 exhibit — the most extensive ever — naturally caught the public's attention. Reviews of its London showing speak of the exhibit's rescuing Lear from "obscurity," especially his career as an artist. Although most reactions to his paintings are positive, one reviewer at least was not as enthusiastic as most. As I have mentioned earlier, Michael Patrick Hearn in "How Pleasant Is It to Know Mr. Lear?" dwells upon Lear's periodic dislike of painting, his "lack of joy," and suggests that this discomfort is evident "everywhere in his landscapes in oil." Hearn continues his criticism by agreeing with those, like Runciman, who believe that Lear is not capable of representing the human figure. Hearn writes that Lear "knew little about the human anatomy" (6). He also finds fault with the oils for their poor sense of color and for their "lack of a spatial depth" (26). Furthermore he is impatient with what he calls the over-worked canvases. As Hearn says, Lear "just did not know when to stop." Hearn is also disappointed with the Tennyson illustrations: "The results seem hardly worth the effort that went into" them (27).

Christopher Neve's review, "The Artist Who Hated His Nose," in *Country Life* (1985) is more laudatory and speaks of "the beautiful, steely, flexing, precise line" in Lear's drawings and paintings (1267). Neve believes that Lear "must have been among the best topographical draughtsmen in a period of many adventurous travel artists." Unlike most critics, Neve regards the larger oils with enthusiasm.

In another review, "Edward Lear and the Pre-Raphaelite Impossibility: Reflections on the Lear Exhibit: The National Academy of Design, New York, September 10-November 3, 1985," Ann C. Colley dwells upon the paintings on display that were executed under William Holman Hunt's instruction. In the essay she describes their work together and suggests that Lear's particular style — his interest in depicting landscape for its own sake, rather than for its allegorical significance; his refusal to celebrate the human figure (or, at least, to subordinate the landscape to it); his preference when he was not following Hunt's example for emphasizing the leading topographical lines rather than filling in all the details — did not ultimately predispose him to accept the Pre-Raphaelite principles. In an earlier article, "Edward Lear and Thomas Seddon: The Paradox of Inquiry" (1984), Colley also touches upon Lear's relationship with the Pre-Raphaelites.

The 1986 Royal Academy Exhibition was certainly the most extensive but not the only one mounted in the 1980s. In 1983, for instance, the Fine Art Society (London) displayed a number of watercolors, drawings, and some oils. In reviewing the exhibit for *Country Life* (1985) Rosemary Hill speaks of these selections' "freshness and immediacy" in spite of the fact that Lear was not an "innovative" artist. She remarks on his indebtedness to the landscapes of Claude Lorrain, points out his tendency to engage the "grand view, the widest, emptiest horizon," and notes his passion for detail. She finds, as a consequence, that the oils are "ponderous." Another indication of a growing interest in Lear's paintings in the 1980s is Raymond Lister's including Lear in his book *British Romantic Painting* (1989). In the section on Lear, Lister describes him as "an excellent landscape painter in oil and watercolour" and points out Lear's habit of writing mnemonic notes on his sketches. Significantly, though, Lister pays more attention to the natural history prints. For them he reserves his highest praise. He goes so far as to exclaim, "The startling beauty of his bird sketches takes them into the sphere of the Sublime ..." (15).

In the 1990s once more it is Vivien Noakes who is instrumental in bringing together materials and making them accessible to the reading public. Noakes's *The Painter Edward Lear* (foreword by H R H The Prince of Wales), published in 1991, assembles drawings, watercolors, and oil paintings from the entire span of Lear's artistic career (including several childhood pieces) and talks about each in detail. She discusses the tradition of the topographical artist; she describes Lear's various techniques of producing his art work; and she mentions the artists who inspired him. Resuming the point of view she expressed in her 1968 biography of Lear, Noakes once more indicates her preference for the watercolors. Her remarks exemplify the predominant criticism:

> ... the spiritual understanding which animated his watercolours slipped beyond his grasp when he was constrained indoors in his studio. This sense of removal from the spirit of nature which gave a powerful dimension to his watercolors, combined with his lack of technical mastery and his belief that a reputation could be made only by the exhibition of large and imposing oil paintings, led to the creation of grandiose pictures, many of which lack the quiet passion which characterises so much of his watercolour work. (9)

In this comprehensive and beautifully illustrated book Noakes also describes the studio spaces in which Lear painted and discusses his working habits (his refusal to be idle), his way of selling his work or of approaching a patron, his mode of traveling to places where he painted, and his responses to the various reviews of his canvases. In a helpful appendix Noakes documents his sales and exhibits of individual works.

At one point in her book, Noakes poses an important question: why has it taken so long to establish Lear's reputation as a painter? In her answer, she suggests that his turning his back on "fashionable subject matter," his less than strong technical powers, his problems with his eyesight, and his dependency upon patronage are contributing factors. All these elements, she suggests, cut into his creative powers and encouraged him to take refuge within a conservative tradition.

There will obviously be more criticism of the art in the future, for his paintings continue to be exhibited. For instance, from February to April in 1991 the National Galleries of Scotland mounted an exhibit of the "Drawings by Edward Lear from the Collection of the Honorable Sir Steven Runciman." Moreover, Lear's paintings now hang as part of permanent collections — they are not displayed only during special events. One of his oils, for example, hangs at the Yale Center for British Art among those done by the established painters — a sign that Lear has become a major nineteenth-century figure.

The Music

The reception of Lear's musical settings of poems has usually been a warm one. His audiences, who after dinner parties or at spontaneous moments listened to Lear accompany himself on the piano while he sang, are reported to have wept over his sentimental renditions and laughed uproariously at his humorous ones. Some of Lear's most popular songs are based upon his own nonsense verses like "The Pelican" and "The Yonghy-Bonghy-Bò." In "Yonghy-Bonghy-Bò: I. The Poem. II. The Music," Philip Hofer and the

American composer Randall Thompson (*Harvard Library Bulletin*, 1967) discuss the poem and its musical setting. In the first section Hofer remarks upon the changes between the holograph manuscript and the final version. In the second Thompson discusses the three musical versions, two arranged by Professor Pomè, in the Houghton Library. Thompson opens his section by reminding his readers how difficult it is to set down someone else's melody:

> Anyone who has written down an untutored composer's tune from his singing of it, phrase by phrase, knows how difficult it is to note it accurately. The inventor of the tune rarely if ever sings it twice the same way; when he begins over again somewhere in the middle, both the notes and the rhythm are likely to vary each time, sometimes widely; and if pressed, he often does not know which version he intended or prefers. At such moments, perhaps secretly intimidated by the erudition of his amanuensis, the author of the tune will hopefully let him decide what is "best." (231)

Thompson suggests that the page-proof version of the melody is Lear's, for it is riddled with errors and lacks such necessary items as a time-signature. Knowing his musical inadequacies, Lear must have given the melody to Professor Pomè. But more problems enter, for when Professor Pomè adds harmony, the metrical pattern alters the original intent; moreover, notes that perhaps Lear did not want to include are introduced.

Thompson speaks of the music's style as that of "a drawing-room ballad" (223) and describes its musical structure. In his discussion, he illustrates how the structure complements the poem's sentiments and how its musical expressions mirror or offer an ironically humorous twist to the words they are expressing. Thompson concludes his article by suggesting that Lear, who was a passionate lover of music, "felt that the greatness of a piece of music could easily be measured by the quantity of tears it caused to flow. If his setting of the Bò's courtship is tearful, it is because he liked that kind of music." Thompson adds, "He could clown in his verses: in his music he was in earnest. The nonsense words gave him positive pleasure: the sad music voiced the pity rooted in his heart. Through the incongruity of the combination of humor and sadness, the song casts its indefinable spell" (237).

Lear's settings of Tennyson's poems also moved his listeners. (Lear had an enormous admiration for Tennyson's poems.) For example, after hearing Lear sing his setting of Tennyson's "Home they brought her warrior dead," Archbishop Campbell Tait, later Archbishop of Canterbury, was so taken by what he had heard that he exclaimed, "Sir! You ought to have half the Laureateship!" These songs are the subject of Anne Henry Ehrenpreis's "Edward Lear Sings Tennyson Songs" (1979). In her article Ehrenpreis, using letters and diaries, gathers the reactions of Lear's contemporaries. She gives a history of the twenty-one pieces that were published and lists those that seem to have remained unpublished. In her discussion she makes the interesting point that in Lear's experience there was always "a thin edge between tears and laughter," for at one moment Lear would be singing in tears — with all seriousness — and the very next caught up in parodying his own sentimentality. Ehrenpreis draws a parallel between Lear's painting and his music, for, by and large, in both he was self-taught. Apparently he received little musical training.

In the 1980s another musician analyzed Lear's music. In "Edward Lear — Composer" (1980), after introducing the reader to the fact of Lear's composing settings for poems and after giving a partial list of the compositions, both published and unpublished, I. A. Copley evaluates the music. Acknowledging that Lear was not trained and, therefore, relied upon others to copy down what he played, Copley admits that it is difficult to judge the music, for one never knows what is Lear's and what is the transcriber's emendations. Copley does suggest, though, that the songs remind him of "the more unsophisticated efforts of the pre-Schubertian 'Lied' composers." He then remarks that when Lear "attempts the grand dramatic gesture the results" would "probably strike a 20th century auditor as pathetic at best and decidedly comic at worst" (9). Copley also describes Lear's melodic patterns which he says are based

> mainly on stepwise movement varied by occasional leaps through the notes of a chord. Occasionally the mediant is stressed and he had a decided fondness for a cadence figure wherein the melodic line moves by leaps upwards from the dominant to the mediant and then hence by steps down to the tonic. (39)

Lear, as we have seen, sometimes set his own verses to music, and others have done the same. In 1887, for instance, a reviewer of Lear's *A Book of Nonsense* for *The Spectator* speaks of several of these compositions. He writes:

> We have spoken above of the melodiousness of Mr. Lear's verses, a quality which renders them excellently suitable for musical setting, and which has not escaped the notice of the author himself. We have also heard effective arrangements, presumably by other composers, of the adventures of the Table and the Chair, and of the cruise of the Owl and the Pussycat, — the latter introduced into the "drawing-room entertainment" of one of the followers of John Parry. (1251)

The reviewer then wonders why "in these days of adaptation ... no enterprising librettist has attempted to build a child's comic opera out of the materials supplied" in the "nonsenses" (1251).

The reviewer could not have foreseen that in the twentieth century Virgil Thomson would write a cantata based on the poems of Lear (1976); that Peter Westergaard would write a chamber opera entitled *Mr. and Mrs. Discobbolos* (1968); that Igor Stravinsky, late in his life, would compose a setting for "The Owl and the Pussycat" (1967); and that Roberto Gerhard would compose "The Akond of Swat, for Voice and Percussion" (1975). And there are more. For instance, listening to my car radio I suddenly found myself hearing the King Singers performing Goffredo Petrassi's settings (composed in the 1950s) of a few of the limericks. Petrassi used Italian translations. The music that the 1887 reviewer says he hears within Lear's verses continues to sound.

4: The Letters and Journals

> *Every human being capable of writing ever since the invention of letters must have written to me, with a few exceptions, perhaps, such as the prophet Ezekiel, Mary Queen of Scots, and the Venerable Bede.*

> *I abhor the sight of a pen, and if I were an angel I would immediately moult all my quills for fear of their being used in calligraphy.*

IN ADDITION TO ILLUSTRATING, painting, and creating nonsense verses and stories, Lear spent considerable time composing letters — sometimes thirty-five before breakfast — and writing his travel journals.

The Letters

Not all of his letters have, of course, survived. But a sufficient number have so that a reader of them can easily get a sense of Lear's intermittently wandering life as well as his manner of relating to family members, close friends, acquaintances, and prospective buyers of his paintings. These letters often reveal the loneliness that was not far below the surface of his playful prose. Occasionally these letters also offer glimpses of how Lear reacted to certain social or political matters. And, of course, they are often full of his nonsense — his drawings, his limericks, his comical spellings. His letters to Chichester Fortescue, or "40scue," often shift quite abruptly into the nonsensical mode. In a February 15, 1859 letter to Fortescue, Lear, writing from Rome, wonders whether "there is likely to be war or not" and then jumps quickly to his humorous complaints about a lady residing in the apartment beneath him. Using the nonsense both to mask and reveal his annoyance with her, he grumbles:

> A vile beastly rottenheaded foolbegotten brazenthroated pernicious piggish screaming, tearing, roaring, perplexing, splitmecrackle crashmecriggle insane ass of a woman is practising howling belowstairs with a brute of a singingmaster so horribly, that my head is nearly off. (*Letters of Edward Lear,* 132)

All his letters are intimate, fluent, and what he might call "spongetaneous."

There are three editions of the correspondence. The first, edited by Lady Strachey, appeared in 1907 (*Letters of Edward Lear*); the second, also edited by Lady Strachey, was published in 1911 (*Later Letters of Edward Lear to Chichester Fortescue and Frances Countess Waldegrave*). The third is Vivien Noakes's 1988 edition, *Edward Lear: Selected Letters*.

In the first edition Lady Strachey, the niece of Chichester Fortescue and Lady Waldegrave, explains that she has collected these letters written between 1847 and 1864 to give readers a better sense of the person who wrote the nonsense verses, for, as she points out, "practically to none is known the depth of character and personality of the man who wrote" them (xiii). The letters, she writes, "show the man in every possible vein of humour, both grave and gay, and also show forth a most lovable personality" (xiv). Lady Strachey also wants to give the readers "some idea of his real life-work" — his paintings — so she includes not only an essay by Henry Strachey appraising them but also reproductions of various watercolors and sketches done by Lear during his travels.

This 1907 edition of the letters seems to have given people delightful reading. For instance, G. K. Chesterton in "How Pleasant to Know Mr. Lear" (1908) speaks of them as being "full of broad English fun, full of splendid English high spirits" (122). A few other reviewers, however, are, perhaps, less ebullient, like the one writing for the December 14, 1907 issue of *The Athenaeum* who worries about the correctness of the modern Greek Lear often interspersed in his letters. The reviewer, however, praises Lear for his sense of friendship. He writes, "Lear himself was, as he believed, debarred from love by ugliness; but he was a true friend, and was never jealous of others who enjoyed happiness which he thought denied to himself" (761).

Lady Strachey's 1911 edition of the correspondence continues to offer a closer look at Lear's personality and to introduce more of his watercolor sketches and drawings to the public. The preface written by Hubert Congreve, a long-time younger friend of Lear's, adds to the sense of immediacy that Lear's letters give. Congreve's affectionate biographical narrative mirrors the charm, the humor, and the vivacity of the volume's contents.

This 1911 edition of the letters was also well received. Walter Jerrold in "One of the Great Masters" (1911) speaks of the edition as a further revelation of the character of the writer of those [nonsense] books, a further addition to the shelves on which we keep the letters of Lamb, FitzGerald and the rest of that small company of correspondents who, writing for the few, delight the many. (148)

Jerrold suggests that this edition secures Lear's reputation as a "letter-writer." He also remarks that "although there is much of delightful nonsense in these letters, there is much else as well, in the way of anecdotes and reminiscences of notable people, and many touches on serious subjects which show once more that the true humorist is a man who thinks and feels deeply ..." (150).

The reviewer for the December 9, 1911, issue of *The Academy* also enjoys the letters. He remarks not only upon the nonsensical passages that make the letters "wholly delightful" but also upon what the letters reveal about Lear's industrious dedication to his work as an artist. He writes:

Lear was an indefatigable landscape-painter. He believed in hard work and hated idlers. The wonder is that, seeing he devoted so much time to art, he should have had a free hour in which to write letters. He must have regarded letter-writing as a happy form of relaxation. (6)

After the publication of the 1907 and 1911 editions the letters continued to interest critics. In his 1924 essay, "Edward Lear," Maurice Baring identifies two reasons why the letters capture people's attention: "First of all they reveal Lear's character, and enrich the world with fresh examples of his unique humour; and secondly, since Lear had a large number of friends, they paint the period" (257). For Baring the charm of the correspondence is its "absolute naturalness" (250). He admires Lear's gift "of relating trivial incidents of everyday life." It is this quality, according to Baring, that is "the greatest charm of letter writing" (250).

Another critic who discusses the 1907 and 1911 editions of the letters is R. L. Mégroz. In his 1938 article, "The Master of Nonsense," which he wrote for *The Cornhill Magazine*, Mégroz discovers in the letters a person who "was divided between work and the claims of friendship" and who "gave himself without stint to both" (176). The letters reveal, according to Mégroz, "a lovable person who worked hard and suffered much from melancholy" (176).

With all this attachment to Lady Strachey's editions of the correspondence and with a growing curiosity about Lear's biography, it is really quite remarkable that a new edition of letters did not appear until over seventy years later. In 1988 Vivien Noakes, who has done so much to make Lear materials available to the public, came out with a new edition and a new selection, *Edward Lear: Selected Letters*. Her edition publishes many letters that are not in Lady Strachey's editions. For instance, she includes letters written when Lear was an adolescent and letters he sent to his other family members throughout his life. The selection ranges from a letter written on January 17, 1826 (when Lear was fourteen) — some of the early letters are written in verse — to one written on November 29, 1887, just two months before his death on January 24, 1888.

In her introduction to *Selected Letters,* Noakes asserts that Lear did not write his letters for posterity. They are, instead, the "unselfconscious setting down of his responses to what he saw and experienced" (xi). They show, Noakes believes, the range of his friendships and the warmth he had for children. She suggests that the letters are fascinating for what they do not include. For instance, there is merely one indirect reference to epilepsy, an illness that plagued him throughout his life and affected his sense of himself and his relationships with other people (xi). She remarks on how much the letters show Lear's love of words and their sounds, his enthusiasm for traveling and seeing new places, and his preoccupation with his financial problems.

In an instructive section Noakes also describes Lear's diurnal practice of writing letters and, interestingly enough, speaks of his occasional problems with procrastination. Contrary to what most readers probably imagine, Lear sometimes had difficulties getting himself to respond to letters he received. Wherever possible Noakes identifies the people named in the correspondence and offers, as an appendix, a "Biographical Register of Correspondents and Persons Frequently Cited." She also includes end notes to help explicate the more elusive sections of the correspondence.

It should be noted that between Lady Strachey's editions and Noakes's compilation, there was in 1965 a selection of letters published in Greece entitled *Lear's Corfu: An Anthology Drawn from the Painter's Letters and Prefaced by Lawrence Durrell.* It is a small selection, composed of extracts rather than complete letters. What distinguishes the edition is the fact that Lawrence Durrell wrote the preface to it. In this preface, Durrell speaks of his indebtedness to Lear in his writing *Prospero's Cell*, and he compliments Lear for his study of the Greek language. Marie Aspioti, the editor of the letters, however, is slightly critical of Lear's attitude toward the people of Corfu, for she points out that he never mentions any of the Corfu intellectuals. Her criticism implies that Lear, like his colonial contemporaries, was not sensitive enough to the life of the people the British ruled.

The Travel Journals

From the moment Lear left England in July, 1837 he kept on moving until he finally settled in San Remo, Italy in 1870. Even then, between 1873 and 1875, and in his sixties, he left his home to make an ambitious tour of India. Lear had never been content sitting still. He once wrote, "No life is more *shocking* to me than sitting motionless like a petrified gorilla as to my body and limbs hour after hour ..." (as quoted in Jackson, xix). He longed to be "far away," even if the mode of travel was uncomfortable and awkward. Lear preferred to travel independently and lightly. In spite of his delicate health, Lear endured such discomforts as cold and draughty inns, insect bites, brushes with cholera, horses that seemed intent upon dislodging him from the saddle, seasickness, imminent revolutions, bandits, and crowds of muslims who did not approve of his creating images (at one point Lear replaced his western hat with a fez so that he might not be easily recognized and stoned). His enthusiasm for all he saw carried him through these difficulties, and so did his humor.

One of the primary reasons Lear traveled was to make drawings and watercolor sketches of distant places like Turkey, Albania, Egypt, the Sinai, Lebanon, and India. He made thousands of sketches and paintings, and, as a consequence, left one of the most extensive records of these countries in the nineteenth century. Lear also went to places more familiar to artists and the public, such as Greece and Palestine. As Vivien Noakes explains in the catalogue accompanying the 1985 Royal Academy Exhibition, Lear, during these travels, liked to:

> wander slowly in a "stopping, prying, lingering mode of travel" ... but when he settled down to work he drew with concentration and speed. These drawings were done in pencil, with often extensive notes about colour and content which would provide the necessary reference for later work back in his studio. He wrote in the location, date and occasionally the time of the drawing, numbering the works in sequence which would begin again when he moved from one country to the next. After his return, he laid in colour washes based on the notes he had made, and "penned out" the pencil drawing and writing in ink, a task which filled winter evenings when the light had gone. (105)

While traveling Lear also kept diaries in which he recorded his impressions of the landscape and events which caught his attention. Sometimes the world of nonsense was not far away. Later he consulted these diaries and wrote up descriptions of his travels for publication. These journals have, perhaps, received more editorial attention than the letters.

Lear published many of his journals during his lifetime. These are *Views in Rome and Its Environs* (1841), *Illustrated Excursions in Italy,* 2 volumes (1846), *Journals of a Landscape Painter in Greece and Albania* (1851), *Journals of a Landscape Painter in Southern Calabria and the Kingdom of Naples* (1852), *Views of Seven Ionian Islands* (1863), and *Journal of a Landscape Painter in Corsica* (1870). All these sold well — there was already an active interest in travel literature — and they received recognition from significant figures. For instance, after seeing the two volumes of *Illustrated Excursions in Italy*, Queen Victoria requested that Lear come and give her drawing lessons, which he did. And after receiving *The Journals of a Landscape Painter in Southern Albania* as a wedding present, Alfred Tennyson composed the poem "To E. L. Upon his Travels in Greece." These journals, of course, won Lear the reputation of being a "seasoned traveller," so when John Murray first put together a *Handbook for Travellers in Greece*, he incorporated Lear's advice about packing. Their contents vary. For instance, two of these published journals, *Views in Rome and Its Environs* and *Views in the Seven Ionian Islands*, are, as their titles suggest, primarily collections of his watercolor sketches. Their texts are not extensive, for the books were published for those English who frequently spent time in these places and who might enjoy looking at pictures of what they have seen or been near. The remaining four published journals, however, contain lengthy, discursive passages about countries that were less familiar or accessible to an English audience. As Noakes explains, these were not travel guides; they were books that described and illustrated "places and ways of life little known to the English." To make her point she draws a helpful analogy between these journals and Lear's animal and bird prints. She writes, "They are in some ways the travel equivalents of the books of natural history to which Lear had contributed, where newly discovered species were also described and illustrated" (*Edward Lear,* 157).

Some of Lear's journals, though, remained unpublished and in the possession of Franklin Lushington who in 1897 introduced and printed a few selections from them in an article for *Macmillan's Magazine*. These passages often reveal Lear's unquenchable humor. For example, in a journal entry written after spending an uncomfortable night in the Hebron Quarantine Building (April 7, 1858) — while waiting for a safe escort into dangerous territory — Lear writes:

> The prolonged night was characterized by the crying of jackals round that dreary quarantine abode. On the previous night a particularly vigorous owl had frequented the building and practised hooting through a hole in the wall.

In his introductory remarks to his article, "A Leaf from the Journals of a Landscape Painter," Lushington not only recalls dramatic and humorous moments in their own travels together but also defends Lear's journals against the supposition that they are full of passages that are merely "vague rhetorical word-painting." Lushington insists that instead the journals are replete with accurate rather than "vague" descriptions. He writes, "They deserve full acceptance as true notes of the vivid impressions conveyed to the sense of the painter during his study of scenery" (411).

Between 1897 and 1938 no new materials about Lear's travels seem to have emerged. In 1938, however, there is some revival of interest in them. In his biography of Lear, for instance, Angus Davidson comments on the published journals, particularly upon their illustrations. He is disappointed that the printed pictures fall "sadly short" of their originals, especially those from Albania and Calabria. He complains:

> They have the harsh, dreary, mechanical look of illustrations in any commonplace guide-book of the period: one place looks very much like another. Lear's admirable sensitiveness of line, his power of expressing atmosphere and space and of reproducing the true character of a scene, which gives charm and distinction to the Albanian and Calabrian drawings — these qualities have disappeared entirely. (178)

In the same year as Angus Davidson's biography, Granville Proby published *Lear in Sicily*, a collection of twenty line drawings — previously unknown — that Lear had made when, between May and July 1847, he had toured with John Joshua Proby, an artist who was also Granville Proby's great uncle. Unlike the illustrations that are published in the various journals, these are cartoons revealing Proby and Lear in awkward or humorous moments during their travels. For instance, the first drawing represents Lear being "attacked by a contiguous cur," another shows him swallowing a large fly, and another depicts "P. and L." being pursued "by a large green fly." In still another P. and L. are having severe difficulties with their horses who often seem to disappear. In his introduction to this gathering of cartoons, Granville Proby makes a few remarks about the relationship between Lear and his grand uncle — the two made three tours together. He also writes a biographical sketch of Proby. In addition to the humorous drawings, Granville Proby includes, as a frontispiece, a watercolor, dated May 22, 1847, signed by both Lear and Proby.

Although the journals that had been published were not ignored in the early part of the twentieth century, they were apparently not taken seriously enough to be reissued until 1952 when Herbert Van Thal put together excerpts from them. In his brief introduction to *Lear's Journals: A Selection*, Van Thal mentions how much he admires their "wit" and how much he appreciates the quality of Lear's travel writing. He also registers the pleasure he takes in "the delectable drawings" sketched during those travels. A year later Ray Murphy edited Lear's Indian journal (*Edward Lear's Indian Journal: Watercolours and Extracts from the Diary of Edward Lear 1873–1875*). This 1953 edition made available Lear's previously unpublished account of his late sketching tour of India. Murphy's introduction focuses on Lear's "magnificently complex" character; he comments on the irony that a person, like Lear, who is physically weak and emotionally vulnerable can be such an intrepid traveler and, indeed, "explorer." Murphy suggests that Lear's "lust for landscape emboldened" him — "The flesh may have been weak but the spirit was steel." Murphy also suggests that Lear traveled to escape his feeling of social discomfort.

In the next decade, three new editions of Lear's journals or accounts of his travels appeared: *Edward Lear in Southern Italy: Journals of a Landscape Painter in Southern Calabria and the Kingdom of Naples* (1964); *Edward Lear in Greece: Journals of a Landscape Painter in Greece and Albania* (1965); and *Edward Lear in Corsica: The Journal of a Landscape Painter* (1966).

In his introduction to the 1964 *Edward Lear in Southern Italy* (a reissuing of the 1852 *Journal of a Landscape Painter in Southern Calabria*) Peter Quennell also remarks on the irony that a gentle, delicate, and epileptic man braved the hazards of difficult travel. The reviewer reading this new edition for the December 3, 1964, issue of *The Times Literary Supplement* admires the writing for its vividness and its personal moments but has difficulty with Lear's neglecting the "obvious imminence of the revolution which eventually curtailed his Calabrian trip" (1105). In 1965 an earlier journal, *Journals of a Landscape Painter in Albania* (1851), was reprinted as *Edward Lear in Greece*, and in 1966 yet another, *Journal of a Landscape Painter in Corsica* (1870) was reprinted as *Edward Lear in Corsica: The Journal of a Landscape Painter*. Obviously, the public's interest in Lear's paintings and travels was reviving. One example of this revival comes in the form of a November 1, 1973, letter to the editor of *Country Life*. The letter is from Mr. and Mrs. Spencer Mills who have just completed a translation into Italian of the *Journal of a Landscape Painter in Southern Calabria (Diario di un Viaggio a Piedi-Calabria)*. The writers disagree with Christopher Neve's opinion that Lear's travels were "mostly uncongenial and disorganized." In his reply, Neve defends his statement by stating that Lear "had not the disposition of the efficient traveller — and is infinitely more attractive and interesting because of it" (1344). He reminds them that Lear's travels in some places were not as smooth or as easy as those in Italy. For instance in Petra his clothes were torn, his beard pulled, and his pockets emptied by bandits. Neve points out that Lear once spoke of having two alternatives: "luxury and inconvenience on the one hand; liberty, hard living and filth on the other ..." (1344). Of these two he chose the latter, for it was the most professionally useful, though not the most agreeable.

More recently interest in Lear's travel journals has grown as the acceptance of his landscape painting has increased. The most recent books are, essentially, art books with lively, interesting commentary. In the 1980s the journals emerge again in a way they had not before. In 1984 Rowena Fowler's

Edward Lear: The Cretan Journal appeared. Taking the text from Lear's diary (now at the Houghton Library, Harvard), Fowler presents a journal that Lear never got around to publishing. In her introduction Fowler discusses Lear's reasons for traveling to Crete, suggests that Lear was aware of the political climate around him, and remarks upon his freedom from the prejudices of what she terms "Romantic philhellenism." She considers his journal writing to be less comprehensive and more personal than that of his contemporaries. She emphasizes that Lear was primarily interested in commenting on the landscape and in the various ups and downs of traveling. Hence, he is "good on people, food, birds, and flowers, disappointing on language, literature and local culture" (12).

In an attempt to distinguish herself from those who only search for clues to Lear's character and personal life, Fowler poses important questions about the relationship between his words and the landscape sketches and the link between his travel writing and the rest of his work. She finds a number of ways in which the journals and the nonsense writing parallel one another: the play with language, the sense of the incongruous, their touch of "social unease and existential despair," and, at times, the feeling of boredom that plagues both Lear on his travels and his nonsense characters, especially when they are being stared at.

In the centenary year of 1988 appeared Philip Sherrard's *Edward Lear: The Corfu Years: A Chronicle Presented Through his Letters and Journals* and Susan Hyman's *Edward Lear in the Levant: Travels in Albania, Greece, and Turkey in Europe 1848-1849*. Both books not only print selections from Lear's letters and journals but also reprint in color many of the paintings Lear did while in these countries. In the introductions, both editors describe the social, historical, and political contexts of these places.

Sherrard's *The Corfu Years* offers a most helpful political history of the island. He also describes the role of the British protectorate in Corfu (it wielded power with little or no check from the English parliament) and Lear's life within that setting (by the time Lear went to Corfu, it had been under British rule for thirty-three years). Sherrard is sensitive to Lear's dependency upon upper-class Englishmen for his livelihood. He prefers to think of him as not quite approving of them. He suggests that Lear "was not a champion of anything and had no desire to dominate" like the colonials. He was both dependent upon, for financial reasons, and independent, for social and political reasons, of the world of upper-class Englishmen (30). In addition to the selections from Lear's writings, Sherrard includes a generous selection of his paintings and sketches. He also includes two appendices. In the first, "Lear as Landscape Painter," he places Lear within the tradition of those artists in pursuit of a "picturesque" landscape who followed the neo-classic romantic conventions. In the second, he identifies the people Lear names in the printed letters and journals.

Hyman's edition of Lear's journal written while traveling in the Levant is also beautifully illustrated. Like others who have reflected upon Lear's strenuous travels, Hyman remarks upon the seeming discrepancy between his ill health and anxious nature and the arduous conditions of his expeditions. In her introduction Hyman talks about the history of his travel writing and his painting. In both she finds that Lear, in his own idiosyncratic way, combines the principles of picturesqueness with absurdity. She speaks of the "counterpoint of the picaresque and the picturesque, the earnestly aesthetic and the absurd" (31). Hyman also lets the reader be more aware of the historical background of the places to which Lear traveled, the tradition in which he was writing, his traveling companions — Charles Church and Franklin Lushington — his interest in the Greek language, and the idiosyncrasies of his style. Hyman thinks of Lear's travel writing as being an "impressionistic" view of what he experienced; she also recognizes the humorous and "modest" elements in it by pointing out those passages in which he records the absurd and funny moments, especially those in which Lear turns the laughter toward himself. She emphasizes that Lear does not choose to include the usual historical or geographical materials that are to be found in other travel writing of the period.

Short pieces or articles on Lear's travels to Greece also appeared in the 1980s. In "Edward Lear in Greece," Eric Glasgow writes about the importance of remembering that Lear was an artist and traveler who through his journals and paintings made his "own special contribution to ... the cultural links between the British people and the people and the land and nature of Greece" (69). In the same year Fari-Maria Tsigahov mentions Lear in her book *The Rediscovery of Greece: Travellers and Painters in the Romantic Era* (1981).

In the 1990s interest in Lear's journals continues. Critics are more and more likely not only to be aware of them but also to have read parts of them. One instance is Alison Rieke's "Stevens in Corsica, Lear in New Haven" which appeared in *The New England Quarterly* (1990). In this article Rieke illustrates how Wallace Stevens when composing his poem "An Ordinary Evening in New Haven" (1949) used Lear's *Journals of a Landscape Painter in Corsica* (1868) as a parallel text or subtext for the poem. In the past, according to Rieke, critics have considered the influence of Shelley, Keats, Hopkins, and Whitman, but none has considered Lear. Rieke develops this idea more thoroughly in the chapter on Lear's influence on Stevens's poetry in her study of nonsense, *The Senses of Nonsense* (1992).

In the future it is to be hoped that more critics will become familiar with the journals and, following Rowena Fowler's lead, think of them as an integral part of his work. There needs to be more thought given to how his journal writing interacts with his painting and his nonsense. In the future there will also be more historical and political commentary now that Philip Sherrard and Susan Hyman have set the examples.

5: Biographers and Collectors

> *How pleasant to know Mr. Lear!*
> *Who has written such volumes of stuff!*
> *Some think him ill-tempered and queer,*
> *But a few think him pleasant enough.*

AS WE HAVE SEEN, some of the most sensitive reactions to Lear's work are embedded within accounts of his life. Because biographies can be an important part of the critical apparatus, I shall offer the reader a brief survey of those written about Lear. The following pages indicate how people since 1888, the year of Lear's death, have chosen to represent him and have, consequently, influenced the manner in which critics have approached his work.

In a sense the earliest biographies of Lear are the obituaries which appeared in magazines like *The Academy, The Athenaeum,* and *The Saturday Review.* In these obituaries the writers seem to place more emphasis on Lear as a "hardworking" and sometimes accomplished artist or travel writer than on his nonsenses. They take for granted their readers' familiarity with the limericks and the poems. In the February 1888 issue of *The Athenaeum,* for instance, the writer of the obituary speaks at length about Lear's sensitivity toward the landscapes he painted and then quickly adds a laudatory sentence about the nonsense and Lear's "infinite humour and keen-edged wit ..." (154). As might be expected these obituaries also dwell upon Lear's personality. The writer for the February 1888 issue of *The Saturday Review,* for example, describes Lear's vitality — "He was a man of striking nobility of nature, fearless, independent, energetic, given to forming for himself strong opinions" (130) — and refers to his generosity and his playfulness. Significantly this writer also mentions the periods of "black depression and nervous irritability" (130) that are to become such an important part of the subsequent biographies.

Even as close to a life as an obituary is, there are mistakes of fact. For instance, the obituary in *The Athenaeum* mistakenly states that Lear "was born on the estate of the Earl of Derby, near Knowsley Hall, Lancashire, the son, we think of one of the late Earl's agents or tenants much employed in and about Prescot" (154–55). (Lear was born to a middle-class family in Holloway.)

Encyclopedias and biographical dictionaries are other early sources. Franklin Lushington's entry on Lear for the 1911 (the famous eleventh edition) of the *Encyclopedia Britannica*, for instance, like the obituaries, emphasizes Lear as an artist and an indomitable traveler rather than as a writer of nonsense. In his discussion of Lear's art work, Lushington reveals his preference for Lear's watercolors. He joins the critics who do not think as highly of the oil paintings. From his point of view, the oil paintings, though "nobly conceived," reveal "some defect of technique or eyesight" that make them "crude or deficient in harmony" (330).

It was not until 1938, though, that the first full-length biography appeared. In a way Angus Davidson's *Edward Lear: Landscape Painter and Nonsense Poet* (reissued in 1950 and 1968) follows the lead of the obituary writers, for it too tends to stress the paintings rather than the nonsense. Although, of course, Davidson devotes a number of chapters to the limericks and poems, there are many more chapters about Lear's career as an artist.

In the opening chapter Davidson dwells upon Lear's childhood and its complexities: Lear's separation from his parents, his problems with bronchitis and asthma, and his epileptic seizures. In the rest of the book Davidson describes Lear's diligent working habits, speaks of his willingness and ability to travel in spite of difficulties with health and traveling conditions, and refers to his various idiosyncrasies. Throughout he is sensitive to Lear's need for friendship and, as a consequence, addresses the question of Lear's relationship to Franklin Lushington — a topic which was to fascinate most subsequent biographers. He suggests that Lear was "strongly attracted" to Lushington, but because "Lear's friendship with Lushington was — on his side — of a deeper, more emotional kind, it was at the same time, owing to Lushington's character, of necessity more reserved" (33). Within this frame of reference Davidson also discusses Lear's ambivalence toward marriage. He concludes that even though Lear seriously considered marriage twice in his life, he had "little interest of the sensual kind in the opposite sex" (160). Davidson tends to think of Lear as a person who, in spite of his large network of friends, was "fundamentally isolated" and as one who was driven by "some deeper disquiet, some hidden and unrecognized anxiety" (93). As a consequence, throughout his adult life he tried to "escape" from his surroundings. He was continuously on the move.

Davidson's portrait of Lear's frequently melancholy and lonely or what Davidson calls Lear's "orphaned" life immediately caught other critics' attention and gave them a means of approaching his work through the biographical details. As we have seen in the survey of the critical reactions to the nonsense, a number of critics have explored the connection between Lear's periodically troubled life and the limericks and poems. For instance, S. A. Nock in "Lacrimae Nugarum: Edward Lear of the Nonsense Verses" (1941) refers to Davidson's biography and reads the nonsense verses as Lear's "emotional biography" (68). According to Nock, the limericks and poems brought Lear a "companionship" that he desperately desired and, furthermore, offered him a means of writing about himself. In particular, the nonsense verses and stories let him live a belated childhood — they are, according to Nock, expressions of Lear's "unlived childhood" (75). Nock emphasizes the fact that Lear rarely enjoyed any parental affection. He "never knew the security, the peace of mind, the satisfaction of either maternal or paternal love in any of its manifestations" (74). Many other critics, of course, think of the nonsense as an escape from the anxieties and troubles that plagued Lear.

When Davidson wrote his 1938 biography, he followed what Vivien Noakes refers to as the "Lear family tradition" (Lear tended to exaggerate the facts of his early life), for he recorded certain details of Lear's childhood that Noakes was later to correct. For instance, Davidson erroneously speaks of the Danish origins of the Lear family name, of the father's incarceration in debtor's prison, and of the tragic fate of some of his sisters after that period. These "traditions" lingered until 1968, so that Philip Hofer's *Edward Lear*, a biographical sketch (with illustrations taken from original materials in the Houghton Library) published in 1962, and Joanna Richardson's *Edward Lear*, a monograph published by the British Council in 1965, also presented these mistakes as facts. For instance, Richardson opens her biography by repeating the story of Lear's supposedly Danish origins:

> He was one of the youngest of the twenty-one children of Ann (née Skerrit) and Jeremiah Lear. Mr. Lear was of Danish origin. "My own name", Edward would explain, "is really LØR, but my Danish Grandfather picked off the two dots and pulled out the diagonal line, and made the word Lear." (9)

The tone of these two publications is similar to Davidson's. Richardson, in particular, emphasizes and elaborates upon Davidson's sense of Lear's loneliness and the difficulties of his childhood. She refers almost immediately to Lear's epilepsy and, like the preceding biographers, mentions his asthma, bronchitis, and poor sight, as well as his painful self-consciousness about his large nose. She, like the others, also dwells upon "the ultimate lack of love" in Lear's life: Lushington's failure to show Lear affection; Lear's conviction that he could not marry; and his "search for temporary forgetfulness" through his travels. Richardson thinks of the limericks as a kind of "release" from these realities.

The most reliable and complete of the biographies, Vivien Noakes's *Edward Lear: The Life of a Wanderer*, was published in 1968. (It was revised in 1979). It is a carefully researched book that not only leads the reader through the particulars of Lear's experiences but also offers a critical appreciation of his work and gives a detailed description of the circumstances under which he conducted his varied career as a writer, painter, and occasional composer. Throughout the book Noakes weaves selections from Lear's letters, journals, and diaries into the text, at times giving the illusion that Lear is writing his own biography.

The book's opening chapters are especially valuable for they address the misunderstandings about Lear's childhood. Explaining that Lear himself exaggerated the truth about his childhood, Noakes corrects the consequent errors. For instance, she informs the reader that Lear's father went bankrupt but never went to debtor's prison; that what Lear says about his Danish origins is "delightful, but quite untrue" (14); that the Lear's never lost their home in Holloway; and that Lear's sisters who were supposed to have died as a consequence of the family's financial problems did not die because of those difficulties. Throughout the rest of the biography, Noakes in the course of her narrative emphasizes Lear's loneliness, attributing it not only to his epilepsy but also to the lack of parental support or love. For instance, when she addresses the question of Lear's sexual preference, she uses his parents' "rejection" of him to explain why he made the choices he did. Speaking perhaps more explicitly than others had so far, she explains that from her point of view Lear "was not a philandering homosexual as some writers have believed him to be. His search was not for physical love, but for someone who would want him as a person in the way that his parents had not wanted him as a child" (132).

The same year as Noakes's biography was published, Davidson's 1938 biography was reissued. The double printing is proof that for many Lear had become, as he had for a reviewer in the *Times Literary Supplement*, "one of the most fascinating and lovable figures of the Victorian age" ("Knowing Mr. Lear,"1358).

Emery Kelen's *Mr. Nonsense: A Life of Edward Lear* (1973) seems to be a biography for a young adolescent audience. Selecting details from the previous biographies, Kelen retells the story of Lear's life in a slightly distorted, fictionalized version. Referring to Lear as a "literary clown and a sad man," he speaks about Lear's separation from his mother, his "ugly" appearance, and, especially, his epilepsy. At one point Kelen uses the fact of Lear's epilepsy to explain why Lear wrote nonsense. In what seems a rather thoughtless moment he writes, "Epileptics are known to like rhymes and repetitions in form and content, and they often form expressions of their own invention" (56–57).

John Lehmann's *Edward Lear and his World*, published in 1977, is a book indebted to other biographical studies, but it distinguishes itself through its numerous illustrations that make Lear's world more tangible and bring the details of his experiences to life. While reading the book one is not sure whether to read or just look at the generous selection of pictures. Lehmann's biography does not contain the biographical errors that can be found in other studies, for it is a well-informed study that discusses, in detail, all aspects of Lear's busy and wandering life. See, for instance, his discussion of the nonsense verses and his account of the purpose and nature of Lear's travels.

Ina Rae Hark's general study for the Twayne Series, *Edward Lear*, published in 1982, includes a section on his life. She too speaks of his loneliness, his fear of rejection, his ambivalence about society and marriage, and his sexuality. Hark, though, suggests that Lear's mixed feelings toward himself and his surroundings, for all their painfulness, constituted a paradox that "became the foundation of his nonsense." She proposes, for instance, that his various childhood traumas, including the possible abuse inflicted by a nineteen-year old cousin, "set the pattern" according to which he lived his life and wrote his nonsense (4).

The most recent of the biographies is Susan Chitty's *That Singular Person Called Lear* (1988). Chitty justifies this "third biography," as she calls it, by claiming that "much more is now known of Lear's immensely complicated personality, and in particular of his homosexuality" (xi). This issue becomes the book's preoccupation. The biography has more of the style, perhaps, of an exposé than a serious study. Interestingly and, I believe, unfairly, Chitty, using the evidence from Lear's and Ann's correspondence, offers the first negative portrait of Lear's sister Ann whom she portrays as a bumbling, fussy, and most unsophisticated — perhaps, slightly foolish — individual. In the end, though, for all its claims the biography does not seem to offer anything new.

Reacting to Chitty's book, Richard Jenkyns in "A Life Lived Backwards" suggests that "to write a life of Lear as a 'Victorian homosexual' is a bit like writing a life of Mrs. Thatcher as a Lincolnshire chemist" (824). According to Jenkyns, Lear's emotional need was above all for friendship. Lear "ached" with loneliness for adults, not children. In uttering these words, Jenkyns is responding to those who read his biography and then think of Lear as being "childish" or suffering from "arrested development" (823-24).

There are also biographical sketches of Lear in several collections of essays. Two interesting examples are Peter Quennell's chapter on Lear in his *The Singular Preference*, a collection of portraits and essays (1952), and a section on Lear in Rupert Croft-Cooke's *Feasting with Panthers: A New Consideration of Some Late Victorian Writers* (1967).

Quennell is interested in identifying the qualities that distinguish Lear from the other Victorian "fantasts" like Richard Doyle and Lewis Carroll. He discovers a number of distinguishing characteristics. First, Lear was "a sociable and bustling extrovert" (95) who loved children, who traveled widely and "worked indefatigably" (96). Second, Lear was also a melancholy person who because he was an epileptic and suffered from asthma and bronchitis never was fully "at ease" in "the world in which he found himself" (96). Quennell also mentions Lear's tendency to protest vehemently and incessantly about such things as noises and to deliver his expressions of annoyance "in a form that reflects as much upon himself as on the condition of the universe" (97). He concludes, however, by emphasizing the "faculty of wonder and the innocence of youth" that permeated Lear's thoughts and overflowed into his nonsense writing.

Quennell's sketch also touches upon the tenacious question of Lear's ambivalence about whether to marry. Quennell believes that because Lear worried so about his health and his finances, and because he feared that if he married he would paint "less and less well" (97), he was, perhaps, relieved to be "celibate" (96).

The subject arises again in Rupert Croft-Cooke's discussion of Lear. This time, however, the emphasis instead of being on Lear's "celibacy" is on his homosexuality. Reacting to Davidson's biography which, according to Croft-Cooke, says "nothing" on the subject of homosexuality, he speculates about whether Lear had any such sexual experiences. He writes:

> Once again the question arises of whether he had any sexual experience at all and it can only be said that if he did so it was with men for he was by nature what Symonds called homogenic. His most percipient biographer Angus Davidson while not minimizing the importance of Lear's friendships says nothing, and perhaps discovered nothing, which suggests they were more than those devoted relationships between men which were common before the emancipation of women made them companions who could be taken on rough and sometimes hazardous excursions abroad such as writers, particularly, loved; before they had any part in political or academic life. (148)

Croft-Cooke then briefly describes Lear's friendship with Franklin Lushington, Chichester Fortescue, George Baring, Giorgio Kokali, Evelyn Baring, Charles Church, and Hubert Congreve.

In addition to these shorter biographical sketches, there are references to Lear's biography in other forms. For instance, there is W. H. Auden's 1939 sonnet:

> Left by his friend to breakfast alone on the white
> Italian shore, his Terrible Demon arose
> Over his shoulder, he wept to himself in the night,
> A dirty landscape-painter who hated his nose.
>
> The legions of cruel inquisitive "They"
> Were so solid and strong, like dogs: he was upset
> By Germans and boats; affection was miles away:
> But, guided by tears, he successfully reached his Regret.
>
> His welcome was prodigious. A flower took his hat
> And bore him off to introduce him to the tongs;
> The demon's false nose made the table laugh; a cat
> Invited him to dance and shyly squeezed his hand;
> Words pushed him to the piano to sing comic songs.
>
> And Children swarmed to him like settlers: He became a land.

And there is Donald Bartheleme's short story "The Death of Edward Lear," published in 1971, that is obviously based upon the biographical studies in the above survey, as Fred Miller Robinson in his article "Nonsense and Sadness in Donald Bartheleme and Edward Lear" (1981) points out. "It is clear" that before writing the story "Bartheleme has read closely about Lear's life." Robinson explains:

> He includes Lear's worries about money and marriage, his attachment to his "many friendships," his unfinished oil painting of Mt. Athos, his song from a text of his "great friend" Tennyson. His Lear dies in his Villa San Remo on January 29, 1888, just as the real Lear did. Bartheleme even includes the detail of Lear's picking up a pen from a bedside table just as he dies. (165)

The story itself is a fictionalized version of Lear's deathbed scene, but it does call up the particulars of his life. Robinson summarizes the story:

> Barthelme begins with the charming fictional conceit of Lear's having sent out invitations to his demise. His friends, who in reality were absent, come to the villa with picnic baskets and children, as if attending a festivity. Lear has chairs arranged in a "rough semicircle" around the bed, as if to seat everyone for a dramatic performance. Then he cries out abruptly, "I've no money! No money!" apologizes for the inconvenience of the hour (the dead of night), indicates his pleasure at

their being there, shrieks, "Should I get married? Get married? Should I marry?" gives short homiletic lectures on Friendship, Cats, and Children ... displays some of his books and watercolors for possible sales, sings a text of Tennyson's, hauls in the enormous oil of Mt. Athos for their perusal, performs "a series of actions the meaning of which was obscure to the spectators" — and finally, at 2:15, the time he announced he would die, he dies. The guests exit, weeping. (165)

In all these biographies Lear emerges as a rather lovable yet grumbling person who was at once surrounded by close friends and admirers, yet isolated and melancholy. The adjectives that often get attached to his name register these seemingly contradictory states of mind: he is "lovable," "amiable," "likeable," "sociable," "affectionate," "full of gusto and humanity," "determined," "diligent," "courageous," "energetic," and "whimsical"; and he is "reticent," "depressed," "gently sad," "lonely," "self-exiled," "ailing," "melancholy," and, most of all, "amiably preposterous."

Although the biographies usually capture these contrasting elements, none succeeds so well as Lear's own self-portraits in bringing these qualities to life. Some of these are his nonsensical drawings of himself as a stout, exuberant, determined, self-conscious, isolated, and, in later years, halting figure propped up by walking sticks. And then there are the autobiographical poems like "How Pleasant to Know Mr. Lear!" and "Incidents in the Life of My Uncle Arly" that in a few stanzas gather together the humor and sadness, the beauty and awkwardness of his life. Rather than quote these better known poems, I shall conclude this survey of the biographies with one that is often overlooked but that vividly represents Lear's character and, furthermore, touches upon his various interests and preoccupations.

Eclogue
Composed at Cannes, December 9th, 1867
[<i>Interlocutors</i> — Mr. Lear and Mr. and Mrs. Symonds]</div>

Edwardus. — What makes you look so black, so glum, so cross?
    Is it neuralgia, headache, or remorse?
Johannes. — What makes you look as cross, or even more so?
    Less like a man than is a broken Torso?
  E.— What if my life is odious, should I grin?
    If you are savage, need I care a pin?
  J.— And if I suffer, am I then an owl?
    May I not frown and grind my teeth and growl?
  E.— Of course you may; but may not I growl too?
    May I not frown and grind my teeth like you?
  J.— See Catherine comes! To her, to her,

    Let each his several miseries refer;
    She shall decide whose woes are least or worst,
    And which, as growler, shall rank last or first.
Catherine. — Proceed to growl, in silence I'll attend,
    And hear your foolish growlings to the end;
    And when they're done, I shall correctly judge
    Which of your griefs are real or only fudge.
    Begin, let each his mournful voice prepare,
    (And, pray, however angry, do not swear!)
 J.— We came abroad for warmth, and find sharp cold
    Cannes is an imposition, and we're sold.
 E. — Why did I leave my native land, to find
    Sharp hailstones, snow, and most disgusting wind?
 J. — What boots it that we orange trees or lemons see,
    If we must suffer from *such* vile inclemency?
 E. — Why did I take the lodgings I have got,
    Where all I don't want is: — all I want not?
 J. — Last week I called aloud, O! O! O! O!
    The ground is wholly overspread with snow!
    Is that at any rate a theme for mirth
    Which makes a sugar-cake of all the earth?
 E. — Why must I sneeze and snuffle, groan and cough,
    If my hat's on my head, or if it's off?
    Why must I sink all poetry in this prose,
    The everlasting blowing of my nose?
 J. — When I walk out the mud my footsteps clogs,
    Besides, I suffer from attacks of dogs.
 E. — Me a vast awful bulldog, black and brown,
    Completely terrified when near the town;
    As calves, perceiving butchers, trembling reel,
    So did *my* calves the approaching monster feel.
 J. — Already from two rooms we're driven away,
    Because the beastly chimneys smoke all day:
    Is this a trifle, say? Is this a joke?
    That we, like hams, should be becooked in smoke?
 E.— Say! what avails it that my servant speaks
    Italian, English, Arabic, and Greek,
    Besides Albanian: if he don't speak French,
    How can he ask for salt, or shrimps, or tench?
 J.— When on the foolish hearth fresh wood I place,
    It whistles, sings, and squeaks, before my face:
    And if it does unless the fire burns bright,

And if it does, yet squeaks, how can I write?
E.—   Alas! I needs must go and call on swells,
That they may say, "Pray draw me the Estrelles."
On one I went last week to leave a card,
The swell was out — the servant eyed me hard:
"This chap's a thief disguised," his face expressed:
If I go there again, may I be blest!
J.—   Why must I suffer in this wind and gloom?
Roomattics in a vile cold attic room?
E. —   Swells drive about the road with haste and fury,
As Jehu drove about all over Jewry.
Just now, while walking slowly, I was all but
Run over by the Lady Emma Talbot,
Whom not long since a lovely babe I knew,
With eyes and cap-ribbons of perfect blue.
J. —   Downstairs and upstairs, every blessed minute,
There's each room with pianofortes in it.
How can I write with noises such as those?
And, being always discomposed, compose?
E.—   Seven Germans through my garden lately strayed,
And all on instruments of torture played;
They blew, they screamed, they yelled: how can I paint
Unless my room is quiet, which it ain't?
—   How can I study if a hundred flies
Each moment blunder into both my eyes?
E. —   How can I draw with green or blue or red,
If flies and beetles vex my old bald head?
J. —   How can I translate German Metaphys-
Ics, if mosquitoes round my forehead whizz?
E. —   I've brought some bacon, (though it's much too fat,)
But round the house there prowls a hideous cat:
Once should I see my bacon in her mouth,
What care I if my rooms look north or south?
J. —   Pain from a pane in one cracked window comes,
Which sings and whistles, buzzes, shrieks and hums;
In vain amain with pain the pane with this chord
I fain would strain to stop the beastly *dis*cord!
E. —   If rain and wind and snow and such like ills
Continue here, how shall I pay my bills?
For who through cold and slush and rain will come
To see my drawings and to purchase some?
And if they don't, what destiny is mine?

>   How can I ever get to Palestine?
> J. —   The blinding sun strikes through the olive trees,
>   When I walk out, and always makes me sneeze.
> E. —   Next door, if all night long the moon is shining,
>   There sits a dog, who wakes me up with whining.
> Cath. — Forbear! You both are bores, you've growled enough:
>   No longer will I listen to such stuff!
>   All men have nuisances and bores to afflict 'um:
>   Hark then, and bow to my official dictum!
>
> For you, Johannes, there is most excuse,
> (Some interruptions are the very deuce,)
> You're younger than the other cove, who surely
> Might have some sense — besides, you're somewhat
>   poorly.
> This therefore is my sentence, that you nurse
> The baby for seven hours, and nothing worse.
>
> For you, Edwardus, I shall say no more
> Than that your griefs are fudge, yourself a bore:
> Return at once to cold, stewed, minced, hashed mutton —
> To wristbands ever guiltless of a button —
> To raging winds and sea, (where don't you wish
> Your luck may ever let you catch one fish?) —
> To make large drawings nobody will buy —
> To paint oil pictures which will never dry —
> To write new books which nobody will read —
> To drink weak tea, on tough old pigs to feed —
> Till spring-time brings the birds and leaves and flowers,
> And time restores a world of happier hours.

Collectors

Many of those who collect Lear's manuscripts, paintings, drawings, and books are also critics. With his many publications discussing Lear's work Philip Hofer, as we have seen, has contributed immensely to scholarship, and so has W. B. Osgood Field (*Edward Lear on My Shelves*), whose collection is now with Hofer's at the Harvard University Library. One collector, Donald C. Gallup, has written a charming account of his efforts to collect Lear materials. I would like to close by mentioning this essay, for it is one that Gallup wrote so that he might be helpful to other Lear scholars. His narrative, "Collecting Edward Lear," appeared in *The Yale University Library Gazette* in 1987. Gallup recounts that his collecting started in the winter of 1943-44 when he was stationed in London. He began by buying small watercolor sketches for very little money. As the years passed, though, Gallup learned that "the Lear market had now passed" him by (129). With the increasing interest in Lear's paintings, the prices naturally went up. Gallup, however, was still able to find pieces in the unusual as well as the more traditional places, so he expanded his collection and began to gather items from all aspects of Lear's work. Like any collector, Gallup talks about missed opportunities and unexpected successes. Because the article gives the reader a good sense of the way Lear's manuscripts, drawings, paintings, and books have sold or been dispersed, it is valuable for any one who wishes to work with original materials or to gain a sense of the history of collecting Lear's work. The sentiment is in Gallup's concluding sentence: "May future viewers and users get as much from my pictures and books as I have received in collecting them!" (142).

6: Conclusion

> *There is a young lady, whose nose,*
> *Continually prospers and grows;*
> *When it grew out of sight, she exclaimed in a fright,*
> *'Oh! Farewell to the end of my nose!'*

LIKE THE YOUNG LADY'S nose, critical responses to Lear's nonsense writing, his natural history studies, his paintings, his journals and letters, and, occasionally, his music prosper with the passing of time. The "nonsenses," as Lear called them, still intrigue critics and kindle ideas about the nature of nonsense itself. The verses and stories continue to be the impetus for readers to think carefully about such matters as language, metaphor, the subconscious, the cultural context, and the relationship between Lear's life and work. Similarly, Lear's writings and art continue to catch the attention of an ever-expanding and appreciative audience. Consequently, rather than growing "out of sight," his varied talents are becoming more visible, even after one-hundred years. The most recent example of this trend is Alison Rieke's study of nonsense, *The Senses of Nonsense* (1992). Even though this study concentrates upon twentieth-century examples, it calls upon Lear's work to develop a theory of nonsense that helps explicate more contemporary texts. In particular it discusses Wallace Stevens's indebtedness not only to Lear's nonsense verses but also to his art, his journals, and his letters.

It is no wonder that Lear's work endures, for it is suggestive. It is, as I mentioned earlier in this study, somewhat elusive. Nothing, no one "umbrella," can quite cover all of it. Some aspect of it will always escape analysis. This factor, I believe, will continue to provoke interesting responses. By releasing critics from the "adult world" of constricting categories and accepted opinions, Lear's verses and drawings will also continue to open up new ways of approaching such subjects as the genre of nonsense or the character of natural history illustration, especially if the critics choose to consider not just one part of Lear's production but rather the work as a whole.

Conclusion

Lear, the nonsense writer, the artist, the traveler, the letter writer, and musician left his readers a legacy of paradoxes with which to play and upon which to reflect. Humor and sentimentality, escape and engagement, conformity and rebellion, for instance, carry on a peaceful battle within his verses and his pictures. It is these seemingly contradictory states that will, in the end, keep his work before the public and engage the critics' lasting attention.

Bibliography: Works by Edward Lear

I: Works of Edward Lear published in his lifetime

Natural History

Illustrations of the Family of Psittacidae, or Parrots. London: Rudolf Ackerman and Edward Lear, 1830–1832.

[Gray, John Edward]. *Gleanings from the Menagerie and Aviary at Knowsley Hall*. Knowsley: Privately Printed, 1846.

Natural History Books to which Lear contributed

The Gardens and Menagerie of the Zoological Society Delineated, edited by Edward Taylor Bennett. Vol. 2. London: John Sharpe, 1831.

Gould, John. *A Century of Birds from the Himalayan Mountains*. London, 1831.

The Transactions of the Zoological Society. Vol. 1. London: Printed for the Society by Richard Taylor, 1833.

Jardine, Sir William and Prideaux John Selby. *Illustrations of British Ornithology*. Vols. 3 & 4. London: Longman, Rees, Orme, Brown, Green & Longman, 1834.

Gould, John. *A Monograph of the Ramphastidae, or Family of Toucans*. London, 1834.

The Transactions of the Zoological Society. Vol. 2. London: Printed for the Society by Richard Taylor, 1836.

Bell, Thomas. *A History of the Testudinata*. London: John van Voorst, 1837.

Gould, John. *A History of British Quadrupeds, including the Cetacea*. London, 1837.

---. *The Birds of Australia and the Adjacent Islands*. London, 1837.

---. *The Birds of Europe.* 5 vols. London, 1832–1837.

---. *Icones Avium.* London, 1837.

Eyton, Thomas Campbell. *A Monograph on the Anatidae, or Duck Tribe.* London: Longman, Orme, Brown, Green & Longman, 1838.

Gould, John. *A Monograph of the Trogonidae, or Family of Trogons.* London, 1838.

Beechey, Capt. Francis. *The Zoology of Captain Beechey's Voyage.* London: Henry G. Bohn, 1839.

Darwin, Charles, ed. *The Zoology of the Voyage of the HMS Beagle.* London, 1841.

Jardine, Sir William, ed., *The Naturalist's Library.* Vols. 2, 4, 9, 18. London, 1843.

Gould, John. *The Birds of Australia.* 7 vols. London, 1840–1848.

Gray, George Robert. *The Genera of Birds.* Vol. 2. London, 1849.

Gray, John Edward, ed. *Tortoises, Terrapins and Turtles.* London, 1872.

Jardine, Sir William. *Illustrations of the Duck Tribe.* Privately printed, n.d.

Nonsense

A Book of Nonsense. London: Thomas McLean, 1846, 1855.

A Book of Nonsense. London: Warne & Routledge, 1861.

A Book of Nonsense. Philadelphia: Willis P. Hazard, 1863.

Nonsense Songs, Stories, Botany and Alphabets. London: Robert Bush, 1871.

The Owl and the Pussy Cat and other Nonsense Songs. Illustrated by Lord Ralph Kerr. London: Joseph Cundall, 1872.

More Nonsense, Pictures, Rhymes, Botany, &c. London: Robert Bush, 1872.

Laughable Lyrics. A Fourth Book of Nonsense Poems, Songs, Botany, Music, &c. London: Robert Bush, 1877.

Travel

Views in Rome and its Environs. London: Thomas McLean, 1841.

Illustrated Excursions in Italy. 2 vols. London: Thomas McLean, 1846.

Journals of a Landscape Painter in Greece and Albania, &c. London: Richard Bentley, 1851.

Journals of a Landscape Painter in Southern Calabria and the Kingdom of Naples. London: Richard Bentley, 1852.

Views in the Seven Ionian Islands. London: Edward Lear, 1863.

Journals of a Landscape Painter in Corsica. London: Robert Bush, 1870.

II: Works by Edward Lear published posthumously

Miscellaneous

Poems of Alfred, Lord Tennyson. Illustrated by Edward Lear. London: Boussod, Valadon & Co., 1889.

Nonsense

Nonsense Books. Boston: Roberts Brothers, 1888.

Nonsense Drolleries. London: Frederick Warne, 1889.

A Nonsense Birthday Book. London: Frederick Warne, 1894.

Nonsense Songs and Stories. Introduction by Sir Edward Strachey. London: Frederick Warne, 1895.

Queery Leary Nonsense, edited by Lady Strachey. London: Mills & Boon, 1911.

The Lear Coloured Bird Book for Children. Foreword by J. St. Loe Strachey. London: Mills & Boon, 1912.

Facsimile of a Nonsense Alphabet Drawn and Written by Edward Lear. London: Frederick Warne, 1926.

Nonsense Songs & Laughable Lyrics, edited by Philip Hofer. Mt. Vernon: Peter Pauper Press, 1935.

The Lear Omnibus, edited by R. L. Mégroz. London: T. Nelson, 1938.

The Complete Nonsense of Edward Lear, edited by Holbrook Jackson. London: Faber & Faber, 1947.

A Nonsense Alphabet. London: H.M.S.O.; New York: Doubleday, 1952.

Teapots and Quails and Other New Nonsenses, edited by Angus Davidson and Philip Hofer. London: John Murray, 1953.

A Drawing Book Alphabet. Cambridge: Harvard College Library, 1954.

Lear Alphabet ABC. London: Constable Young Books; New York: McGraw-Hill, 1965.

Rhymes of Nonsense: An Alphabet. London: Bertram Rota, 1968.

Ye Long Nite in ye Wonderfull Bedde. Cambridge: Friends of the Fitzwilliam Museum, 1972.

St. Kiven and the Gentle Kathleen. Introduction by Donald Gallup. New Haven, 1973.

Lear in the Original, edited by Herman Liebert. London: Oxford University Press, 1975.

A Book of Bosh, edited by Brian Alderson. Harmondsworth, Middlesex: Penguin, 1975.

For Lovers of Birds. Compiled by Vivien Noakes and Charles Lewsen. London: Collins, 1978.

For Lovers of Cats. Compiled by Vivien Noakes and Charles Lewsen. London: Collins, 1978.

For Lovers of Flowers and Gardens. Compiled by Vivien Noakes and Charles Lewsen. London: Collins, 1978,

For Lovers of Food. Compiled by Vivien Noakes and Charles Lewsen. London: Collins, 1978.

A Book of Nonsense. New York: The Viking Press, 1980.

Bosh and Nonsense. London: Allen Lane (Penguin Books), 1982.

The Tragical Life and Death of Caius Marius Esq. ... from Authentic Sauces. New York: Justin G. Schiller, 1983.

Letters

Letters of Edward Lear to Chichester Fortescue and Frances Countess Waldegrave, edited by Lady Strachey. London: T. Fisher Unwin, 1907.

Later Letters of Edward Lear, edited by Lady Strachey. London: T. Fisher Unwin, 1911.

Edward Lear: Selected Letters, edited by Vivien Noakes. Oxford: Clarendon Press, 1988.

Travel

Lear in Sicily. Introduction by Granville Proby. London: Duckworth, 1938.

Edward Lear's Journals: A Selection, edited by Herbert van Thal. London: Arthur Baker; New York: Coward-McCann, 1952.

Edward Lear's Indian Journal: Watercolours and Extracts from the Diary of Edward Lear (1873-1875). London: Jarrolds, 1953.

Edward Lear in Southern Italy. Introduction by Peter Quennell. London: William Kimber, 1966.

Edward Lear in Greece. London: William Kimber, 1964.

Lear's Corfu: An Anthology Drawn from the Painter's Letters. Prefaced by Lawrence Durrell. Corfu: Corfu Travel, 1965.

Edward Lear in Corsica: The Journal of a Landscape Painter. London: William Kimber, 1966.

Edward Lear: The Cretan Journal, edited by Rowena Fowler. Athens: Denise Harvey & Company, 1984.

Views in Seven Ionian Islands: A Facsimile of the Originial Edition Published in 1863 by the Artist. Oldham: Aveyard, Broadbent, 1986.

Edward Lear: The Corfu Years: A Chronicle Presented through his Letters and Journals, edited by Philip Sherrard. Athens: Denise Harvey & Company, 1988.

Edward Lear in the Levant: Travels in Alvania, Greece and Turkey in Europe: 1848-1849, edited by Susan Hyman. London: John Murray, 1988.

Impossible Picturesqueness: Edward Lear's Indian Watercolours, 1873-1875, edited by Vidya Dehejia. Ahmedabad: Mapin Publishing, 1989.

Bibliography: Criticism

Bourjot Saint-Hilaire, A. *Histoire Naturelle des Perroquets*. Paris: F. G. Levrault, 1837–1838.

"Nonsensical Books." *The Saturday Review* (October 5, 1859): 388–89.

Taylor, Tom. *The Times* (June 11, 1860): 76–77.

"Christmas Books II." *The Saturday Review* (December 21, 1861): 646.

"The Science of Nonsense." *The Spectator* (December 17, 1870): 1505–06.

Review of *Nonsense Songs*. *The Saturday Review* (December 24, 1870): 814.

The Examiner, no. 3282 (December 27, 1870): 826.

The Pall Mall Magazine, no. 2117 (November 25, 1871): n.p.

"Mr. Lear's New Nonsense." *The Spectator* (December 23, 1871): 1570–71.

The Times. (December 25, 1871): 4.

"A Book of Nonsense." *Judy, or the London Serio-Comic Journal* (January 18, 1871): 114.

Colvin, Sidney. *The Academy*. 3 (January 15, 1872): 23–24.

The Athenaeum (January 13, 1873): 43.

Review of *Laughable Lyrics*. *The Athenaeum*, no. 2528 (November 18, 1876): 604.

"Current Literature: Christmas and Gift Books." *The Spectator* (December 2, 1876): 1516–17.

"Christmas Books." *The Saturday Review* (December 9, 1876): 734.

Ruskin, John. *The Pall Mall Magazine* (February 15, 1886): n.p.

"Word Twisting *versus* Nonsense." *The Spectator* (April 9, 1887): 492–93.

"Lear's Nonsense Books." *The Spectator* (September 17, 1887): 1251–52.

"Edward Lear." *The Saturday Review* (February 4, 1888): 130.

"Mr. Edward Lear." *The Athenaeum,* no. 3145 (February 4, 1888): 154–55.

"A Humorous Letter Writer." *The Academy.* no. 823 (February 11, 1888): 97.

"Lear's Book of Nonsense." *The Saturday Review* (March 24, 1888): 361–62.

[Strachey, Edmund]. "Nonsense as a Fine Art." *The Quarterly Review.* 167 (October, 1888): 335–65.

"Nonsense Pure and Simple." *The Spectator* (November 3, 1888): 1503–05.

"Sir Edward Strachey on Nonsense." *The Spectator* (November 10, 1894): 638–39.

Lushington, Franklin. "A Leaf from the Journals of a Landscape Painter." *Macmillan's Magazine* 75 (April, 1897): 410–30.

Review of *Letters of Edward Lear to Chichester Fortescue. The Athenaeum,* no. 4181 (December 14, 1907): 760–61.

Strachey, Henry. "Appreciation of Lear as a Painter." *Letters of Edward Lear to Chichester Fortescue and Frances Countess Waldegrave,* edited by Lady Strachey, xxxvi–xl. London: T. Fisher Unwin, 1907.

"A Humorous Letter-Writer." Supplement to *The Academy* (December 9, 1911): 5–6.

Jerrold, Walter. "One of the Great Masters." *The Bookman* (December, 1911): 148–50.

Lushington, Franklin. "Lear, Edward." In *The Encyclopaedia Britannica* Vol. 16. New York: The Encyclopaedia Britannica Company, 1911.

Huxley, Aldous. *On the Margin.* London: Chatto & Windus, 1923.

Baring, Maurice. *Punch and Judy & Other Essays.* London: William Heinemann, 1924.

Cammaerts, Emile. *The Poetry of Nonsense.* London: George Routledge & Sons, 1925.

Reed, Langford. *The Complete Limerick Book.* New York: G. P. Putnam's Sons, 1925.

Malcolm, Ian. *The Pursuit of Leisure, & Other Essays.* London: Ernest Benn, 1929.

Hardie, Martin. "Edward Lear." *Artwork* 6 (1930): 114–19.

Darton, F. J. Harvey. *Children's Books in England: Five Centuries of Social Life.* London: Cambridge University Press, 1932.

Journal of the Royal Institute of British Architects 39 (February 6, 1932): 252.

Osgood Field, William B. *Edward Lear on my Shelves.* New York: Privately Printed, 1933.

"Exhibition and Sales." *Antiques* 26 (July, 1934): 26.

Kent, Muriel. "The Art of Nonsense." *The Cornhill Magazine* 149 (1934): 478–87.

Leimert, Erika. "Die Nonsense-Poesie von Edward Lear (Ein Beitrag zür Psychologie des englischen Humors)." *Neuren Sprache* 45 (1937): 368–73.

Davidson, Angus. *Edward Lear: Landscape Painter and Nonsense Poet: 1812-1888.* Harmondsworth: Penguin Books, 1950. (first published by London: John Murrary, 1938.)

Mégroz, R. L. "The Master of Nonsense." *The Cornhill Magazine* 157 (1938): 175–90.

Staley, Allen. "The Painter of Topographical Poetry." In *Impossible Picturesqueness: Edward Lear's Indian Watercolours, 1873-1875,* edited by Vidya Dehejia. Ahmedabad: Mapin Publishing , 1939.

Nock, S. A. "Lacrimae Nugarum: Edward Lear of the Nonsense Verses." *Sewanee Review* 49 (1941): 68–81.

"Edward Lear at the Redfern Gallery." *Apollo* 35 (1942): 97–98.

Jackson, Holbrook, ed. *The Complete Nonsense of Edward Lear.* London: Faber and Faber, 1947.

Reade, Brian. *An Essay on Edward Lear's Illustrations of the Family of Psittacidae or Parrots.* London: Pion, 1978. (First edition published by Gerald Duckworth, 1949.)

Andersen, Jørgen. "Edward Lear and the Origins of Nonsense." *English Studies* 31 (1950): 161–66.

Bowra, C. M. *The Romantic Imagination.* London: Oxford University Press, 1950.

Brockway, J. T. "Edward Lear, Poet." *Fortnightly Review* 167 (1950): 334–39.

Orwell, George. "Nonsense Poetry." In *Shooting an Elephant and Other Essays.* London: Secker and Warburg, 1950.

Partridge, Eric. "The Nonsense Words of Edward Lear and Lewis Carroll." In *Here, There and Everywhere. Essays Upon Language.* 2d. ed., rev., 162–88. London: Hamish Hamilton, 1950.

Quennell, Peter. *The Singular Preference: Portraits & Essays.* London: Collins, 1952.

Sewell, Elizabeth. *The Field of Nonsense.* London: Chatto and Windus, 1952.

Chesterton, G. K. "How Pleasant to Know Mr. Lear." In *A Handful of Authors: Essays on Books and Writers*, edited by Dorothy Collins. London: Sheed and Ward, 1953.

Legman, Gershon [George Alexander]. *The Limerick: 1700 Examples, with Notes, Variants, and Index.* Paris: Hautes Études, 1953.

Murphy, Ray, ed. *Edward Lear's Indian Journal: Watercolours and Extracts from the Diary of Edward Lear (1873–1875).* London: Jarrolds, 1953.

Sitwell, Sir Sacheverell, Handasyde Buchanan and James Fisher. *Fine Bird Books: 1700–1900.* London: Collins, 1953.

The Burlington Magazine 100 (1958): 295.

Shipp, Horace. "Current Shows and Comments." *Apollo* (July, 1958): 48.

Whittet, G. S. "London Commentary." *The Studio* 156 (1958): 124–26.

Hildebrandt, Rolf. "Nonsense-Aspekte der englischen Kinderliteratur." Ph.D. diss. Hamburg, 1962.

Hofer, Philip. *Edward Lear.* New York: Oxford University Press, 1962.

"In the Galleries." *The Connoisseur* 151 (1962): 49.

Bury, Adrian. "The Other Side of Edward Lear." *Antique Collector* (August, 1963): n. p.

Liede, Alfred. *Dichtung als Spiel: Studien zur Unsinnspoesie an den Grenzen der Sprache.* 2 Vols. Berlin: Walter de Guyter & Co, 1963.

Artmann, H. C. *Edward Lears Nonsense-Verse. Aus dem englischen übertragen.* Frankfurt: Insel-Verlag, 1964.

Lambourne, Maureen. "Birds of a Feather: Edward Lear and Elizabeth Gould." *Country Life* (June 1964): n.p.

Nixon, Howard M. "The Second Lithographic Edition of Lear's Book of Nonsense." *British Museum Quarterly* 28 (1964): 7–8.

Quennell, Peter. Introduction to *Edward Lear in Southern Italy*. London: William Kimber, 1964.

"Travelling Learily." *Times Literary Supplement*. (December 3, 1964): 1105.

Chesterton, G. K. "A Defence of Nonsense." In *Chesterton's Stories Essays, & Poems*. London: Dent, 1965.

Davis, Frank. "Lost Tension in the Auction Room." *Country Life* 138 (November 4, 1965): 1184–85.

Fischer, Grete. *Wie nett, Herrn Lear zu kennen. Reime und Geschichten von Edward Lear ins Deutsche übertragen*. Frankfurt: Heimeran Verlag, 1965.

Richardson, Joanna. *Edward Lear*. London: Longmans, Green & Co., 1965.

Serra, Cristóbal. "Dos principes del absurdisimo inglés: Edward Lear-Lewis Carroll." *Papeles de son Armadans* 39 (1965): 59–64.

Burrows, Miles. "Scroo! Scroo! Scroo!" *New Statesman* 71 (January 7, 1966): 18.

Gray, Donald J. "The Uses of Victorian Laughter." *Victorian Studies* 10 (December 1966): 145–76.

Baring-Gould, William S. *The Lure of the Limerick*. New York: Clarkson N. Potter, 1967.

Hofer, Philip. *Edward Lear as a Landscape Draughtsman*. Cambridge: The Belknap Press of Harvard University, 1967.

Hofer, Philip and Randall Thompson. "The Yonghy-Bonghy-Bò: I. The Poem. II.The Music." *Harvard Library Bulletin* 15 (1967): 229–37.

Croft-Cooke, Rupert. *Feasting with Panthers*. New York: Holt, Rinehart and Winston, 1968.

"Knowing Mr. Lear." *Times Literary Supplement* (December 5, 1968): 1358.

Noakes, Vivien. *Edward Lear: The Life of a Wanderer*. Glasgow: William Collins Sons & Co, Ltd., 1968. (Fontana Paperback, 1979).

Parisot, Henri. *Edward Lear: Limericks et autres poèmes ineptes*. Paris: Mercure de France, 1968.

Maas, Jeremy. *Victorian Painters*. New York: Putnam, 1969.

Davis, Frank. "Putting a High Price on Nonsense." *Country Life*. 147 (January 15, 1970): 118–19.

Hofer, Philip. Introduction to *Edward Lear in Greece: A Loan Exhibition from the Gennadius Library, Athens*. The International Exhibitions Foundation, 1971–1972.

Morris, Edward. "The Beausire Collection of English Watercolours." *The Connoisseur* 707 (1971): 1–9.

Christopher, J. R. "Three Notes on Edward Lear." *Unicorn: An Independent Miscellaneous Journal* 2 (Spring 1972): 13–16.

Petzold, Dieter. *Formen und Funktionen der englischen Nonsense-Dichtung im 19. Jahrhundert.* Nuerenberg: Verlag Hans Carl, 1972.

"Edward Lear's Travels." *Country Life* 154 (November 1, 1973): 1343–44.

Kelen, Emery. *Mr. Nonsense: A Life of Edward Lear.* Nashville: Thomas Nelson, 1973.

Miller, Edmund. "Two Approaches to Edward Lear's Nonsense Songs." *The Victorian Newsletter*, no. 44 (Fall 1973): 5–8.

Neve, Christopher. "There Was a Young Person of ... Edward Lear's Parrots." *Country Life* 153 (April 5, 1973): 899–900.

Reichert, Klaus. *Lewis Carroll Studien zum Literarischen unsinn.* Munich: Carl Hanser Verlag, 1974.

Bailey, Colin J. "Edward Lear at Knowsley." *Apollo* 101 (1975): 394.

Jackson, C. E. *Bird Illustrators: Some Artists in Early Lithography.* London: H. F. & G. Witherby, 1975.

Liebert, Herman W. *Lear in the Original: Drawings and Limericks by Edward Lear for his Book of Nonsense.* New York: H. P. Kraus, 1975.

Benayoun, Robert. *Le nonsense de Lewis Carroll à Woody Allen.* Balland, 1977.

Byrom, Thomas. *Nonsense and Wonder: The Poems and Cartoons of Edward Lear.* New York: E. P. Dutton, 1977.

Enzensberger, Hans Magnus. *Edward Lears Kompletter Nonsensins Deutsche geschmuggelt.* Frankfurt: Insel, 1977.

Lehmann, John. *Edward Lear and his World.* London: Thames & Hudson, 1977.

Prawer, S. S. "The Case of Comrade Lear." *Times Literary Supplement.* (December 23, 1977): 1497.

Greene, David L. Preface to *The Book of Nonsense.* New York: Garland Publishing, Inc., 1978.

Hark, Ina Rae. "Edward Lear: Eccentricity and Victorian Angst." *Victorian Poetry* 16 (Spring-Summer 1978): 112–22.

Ehrenpreis, Anne Henry. "Edward Lear Sings Tennyson Sons." *Harvard Library Bulletin* 27 (1979): 65–85.

"Irresistible Lear." *Country Life* (May 17, 1979): 1527.

Prickett, Stephen. *Victorian Fantasy.* Sussex: Harvester Press, 1979.

Stewart, Susan A. *Nonsense: Aspects of Intertextuality in Folklore and Literature.* Baltimore: John Hopkins University Press, 1979.

Alderson, Brian. "Literary Criticism and Children's Books: or 'Could be Worse'." In *Responses to Children's Literature*, edited by Geoff Fox and Graham Hammond with Susan Amor. New York: K. G. Saur, 1980.

Belknap, George N. "History of the Limerick." *The Papers of the Bibliographical Society of America* 75 (1980): 1–32.

Copley, I. A. "Edward Lear — Composer." *Musical Opinion* 104 (October 1980): 8–9, 12, 39.

Hyman, Susan. *Edward Lear's Birds.* New York: William Morrow and Company, 1980.

Sewell, Elizabeth. "Nonsense Verse and the Child." *The Lion and the Unicorn: A Critical Journal of Children's Literature* 4 (Winter 1980–1981): 30–45.

Willis, Gary. "Two Different Kettles of Talking Fish: The Nonsense of Lear and Carroll." *Jabberwocky: The Journal of the Lewis Carroll Society* 9 (1980): 87–94.

Dotsenko, Rostylav. "Podorozh ukrainu navpaky" (Journey to the Land of Contrariety). *Vsesvit: Literaturno-Mystets'kyi ta Hromads'ko Politychnyi Zhurnal* 12 (December 1981): 188–89.

Glasgow, Eric. "Edward Lear in Greece." In *Salzburg Studies in English Literature: Studies in Nineteenth Century Literature,* edited by Dr. James Hogg, 63-69. Salzburg: Austria, 1981.

Kastner, John. "The Runcible Life and Works of the Remarkable Edward Lear." *Smithsonian* (September 1981): 106-16.

Robinson, Fred Miller. "Nonsense and Sadness in Donald Bartheleme and Edward Lear." *The South Atlantic Quarterly* 80 (1981): 164-76.

Bouissac, Paul. "The Meaning of Nonsense (Structural Analysis of Clown Performances and Limericks)." In *The Logic of Culture: Advances in Structural Theory Methods,* edited by Ino Rossi. London: Tavistock Publications, 1982.

Hark, Ina Rae. *Edward Lear.* Boston: Twayne Publishers, 1982.

Harmon, William. "Lear, Limericks, and Some Other Verse Forms." *Children's Literature: An International Journal. Annual of the Modern Language Association* 10 (1982): 70-76.

Baker, William. "T. S. Eliot on Edward Lear: An Unnoted Attribution." *English Studies: A Journal of English Language and Literature* 64 (December 1983): 564-66.

Hill, Rosemary. "Floating Free: Edward Lear at the Fine Art Society." *Country Life* (November 3, 1983): 1236-37.

Colley, Ann C. "Edward Lear and Thomas Seddon: The Paradox of Inquiry." *The Journal of Pre-Raphaelite Studies* 5 (November 1984): 36-48.

Fowler, Rowena, ed. *Edward Lear: The Cretan Journal.* Athens: Denise Harvey and Company, 1984.

Lambourne, Maureen. "Edward Lear and John Gould." *Antique Collector* (December 1984): n.p.

Bruni Roccia, Gioiella. "Il Problema del Testo Nel *Book of Nonsense* di Edward Lear." *Studi Italiani di Linguistica Teorica ed Applicata* 14 (1985): 219-87.

Maas, Jeremy. "From the Sublime to the Ridiculous." In *Edward Lear:1812-1818 at the Royal Academy of Arts,* edited by Vivien Noakes, 18-19. London: Weidenfeld and Nicolson, 1985.

Neve, Christopher. "The Artist Who Hated His Nose." *Country Life* 177 (May 9, 1985): 1266-67.

Noakes, Vivien, ed. *Edward Lear: 1812-1888 at the Royal Academy of Arts.* London: Weidenfeld and Nicolson, 1985.

Noakes, Vivien. "The Sense and Nonsense of Edward Lear." *Natural History* 94 (December 1985): 58-67.

Ord, Priscilla A. "'There Was an Old Derry Down Derry, Who Loved to Make Little Folks Merry': A closer Look at the Limericks of Edward Lear." *Literary Onomastics Studies* 12 (1985): 93-118.

Runciman, Sir Steven. "Edward Lear." In *Edward Lear: 1812-1888 at the Royal Academy of Arts.* London: Weidenfeld and Nicolson, 1985.

Colley, Ann C. "Edward Lear and the Pre-Raphaelite Impossibility: Reflections on the Lear Exhibit: The National Academy of Design, New York, September 10-November 3, 1985." *The Journal of Pre-Raphaelite Studies* 7 (November 1986): 44-49.

Grassi, Aldo Vittorio. "L'universo nonsensico dei 'limerick' di Edward Lear." *Humanitas: Rivista bimestrale di Culture* 41 (October 1986): 703-18.

Hearn, Michael Patrick. "How Pleasant Is It to Know Mr. Lear." *American Book Collector* 7 (January 1986): 21-27.

Avery, Gillian. "Fantasy and Nonsense." In *The Victorians*. Vol. 6, *The New History of Literature*, edited by Arthur Pollard. New York: Peter Bedrick Books, 1987.

Ede, Lisa. "Edward Lear's Limericks and Their Illustrations." In *Explorations in the Field of Nonsense,* edited by Wim Tigges, 103-16. DQR Studies in Literature, no. 3. Amsterdam: Rodopoi, 1987.

Ede, Lisa. "An Introduction to the Nonsense Literature of Edward Lear and Lewis Carroll." In *Explorations in the Field of Nonsense,* edited by Wim Tigges, 47-60. DQR Studies in Literature, no. 3. Amsterdam: Rodopoi, 1987.

Gallup, Donald. "Collecting Edward Lear." *The Yale University Library Gazette* 61 (1987): 125-42.

Ritvo, Harriet. *The Animal Estate: The English and Other Creatures in the Victorian Age.* Cambridge: Harvard University Press, 1987.

Tigges, Wim. "An Anatomy of Nonsense." In *Explorations in the Field of Nonsense,* edited by Wim Tigges. DQR Studies in Literature, no.3, 23-46. Amsterdam: Rodopi, 1987.

Tigges, Wim. "The Limerick: The Sonnet of Nonsense?" In *Explorations in the Field of Nonsense*, edited by Wim Tigges. DQR Studies in Literature, no. 3, 117-34. Amsterdam: Rodopi, 1987.

van Leeuwen, Hendrik. "The Liason of Visual and Written Nonsense." In *Explorations in the Field of Nonsense,* edited by Wim Tigges. DQR Studies in Literature, no. 3, 61-96. Amsterdam: Rodopi, 1987.

The Bird Illustrated 1550-1900 from the Collection of the New York Public Library. Introduction by Roger Tory Peterson. Text by Joseph Kastner. Commentaries by Miriam T. Gross. New York: Harry N. Abrams, Inc., 1988.

Colley, Ann C. "Edward Lear's Limericks and the Reversals of Nonsense." *Victorian Poetry* 26 (Autumn 1988): 285-99.

Colley, Ann C. "The Limerick and the Space of Metaphor." *Genre* 21 (Spring 1988): 65-91.

Hyman, Susan. *Edward Lear in the Levant: Travels in Albania, Greece and Turkey in Europe: 1848-1849.* London: John Murray, 1988.

Jenkyns, Richard. "A Life Lived Backwards." *Times Literary Supplement.* (July 29-August 4, 1988): 823-4.

Noakes, Vivien, ed. *Edward Lear: Selected Letters.* Oxford: Clarendon Press, 1988.

Pitman, Ruth. *Edward Lear's Tennyson.* Manchester: Carcanet Press, 1988.

Schiller, Justin G., ed. *Nonsensus.* Stroud: Catalpa Press, 1988.

Sherrard, Philip, ed. *Edward Lear: The Corfu Years: A Chronicle Presented through his Letters and Journals.* Athens: Denise Harvey & Company, 1988.

Tigges, Wim. *An Anatomy of Literary Nonsense.* Costerus, n.s. 67. Amsterdam: Rodopi, 1988.

Chitty, Susan. *That Singular Person Called Lear: A Biography of Edward Lear, Artist, Traveller and Prince of Nonsense.* New York: Athenaeum, 1989.

Dehjia, Vidya. *Impossible Picturesqueness: Edward Lear's Indian Watercolours, 1873-1875.* Ahmedabad: Mapin Publishing, 1989.

Lister, Raymond. *British Romantic Painting.* Cambridge: Cambridge University Press, 1989.

Hark, Ina Rae. "The Jew as Victorian Cultural Signifier: Ilustrated by Edward Lear." *Bucknell Review: Journal of Letters, Arts and Sciences* 34 (1990): 82-98.

Rieke, Alison. "Stevens in Corsica, Lear in New Haven." *New England Quarterly: A Historical Review of New England Life and Letters*. 63 (March 1990): 35–59.

Noakes, Vivien. *The Painter Edward Lear*. Newton Abbot: David & Charles, 1991.

Colley, Ann C. "Edward Lear's Anti-Colonial Bestiary." *Victorian Poetry* 30 (Summer 1992): 109–20.

Reike, Alison. *The Senses of Nonsense*. Iowa City: University of Iowa Press, 1992.

Index

The Academy 75, 105
Alderson, Brian 19, 24, 102, 110
American Book Collector 112
Amor, Susan 110
Andersen, Jørgen 14, 106
Anecdotes and Adventures of Fifteen Gentlemen 25-26
Antique Collector 107, 111
Antiques 106
Apollo 53, 59, 60, 107, 109
Artmann, H. C. 16, 107
Aspioti, Marie 76
The Athenaeum 4-5, 12, 74, 84, 104, 105
Auden, W. H. 89-90
Audubon, John James 46, 52
Avery, Gillian 23, 112

Bailey, Colin J. 53, 109
Baker, William 9, 111
Baring, Evelyn 89
Baring, George 89
Baring, Maurice 75, 105
Baring-Gould, William S. 25, 108
Bartheleme, Donald 90
Beardsley, Aubrey 26
Beechey, Capt. Francis 100
Belknap, George N. 26, 110
Bell, Thomas 49, 99
Benayoun, Robert 42, 109
Bennet, Edward Taylor 49, 99
The Birds of Australia and the Adjacent Islands 99
The Birds of Europe 46, 100
A Book of Bosh 102
A Book of Nonsense 2-6, 10, 14, 15, 21, 27, 33, 71, 100, 102
The Bookman 7-8, 105
Bosh and Nonsense 22-23, 102
Bouissac, Paul 27, 43, 111

Bourjot Saint-Hilaire, A. 50, 104
Bowra, C. M. 14, 106
British Museum Quarterly 15, 108
Brockway, J. T. 14, 106
Bruni Roccia, Gioiella 27-28, 111
The Burlington Magazine 60, 107
Burrows, Miles 108
Bury, Adrian 53, 107
Busch, Wilhelm 11
Byrom, Thomas 20, 29, 31, 35, 109

Cammaerts, Emile 8-11, 36-37, 39, 105
Carlingford, Lord 7
Carroll, Lewis 2, 9-11, 16, 22-25, 32, 37, 88
A Century of Birds from the Himalayan Mountains 46, 99
Chesterton, G. K. 8-10, 23, 35-36, 39, 74, 107, 108
Children's Literature 111
Chitty, Susan 88, 113
Christopher, J. R. 18, 109
Church, Charles 82, 89
Church, Fredrich 66-67
Colley, Ann C. 28-29, 30-31, 42, 54-55, 66, 68, 111-14
Colvin, Sidney 104
The Complete Nonsense of Edward Lear 101
Congreve, Hubert 7, 74, 89
Congreve, Thomas 8
The Connoisseur 60, 63, 107, 109
Constable, John 61
Contemporary Review 61
Copley, I. A. 71, 112
The Cornhill Magazine 9-10, 58, 75, 106
Cott, Jonathan 20-21
Country Life 17, 60-61, 67-68, 80, 108, 109-12

"The Courtship of the Yonghy-Bonghy-Bò" 11, 70
Creswick, Thomas 66
Croft-Cooke, Rupert 88-89, 108
Cromer, Lord 7-8
"The Cummerbund" 6

D'Ache, Caran 11
"The Daddy Long-Legs and the Fly" 24
Darton, F. J. 10, 106
Darwin, Charles 100
Davidson, Angus 5, 11-12, 14, 23, 57-59, 85-87, 89, 102, 106
Davis, Frank 17, 61, 108-9
de Bunsen, Madame 5-6
de la Mare, Walter 9-10
Dehejia, Vidya 65, 103, 113
Deleuze, Gilles 32
Derby, Earl of 2, 53
Domin, Andre 26
"The Dong with the Luminous Nose" 6, 11, 18, 35, 45
Doré, Gustaf 11
Dotsenko, Rostyslav 28, 111
Doyle, Richard 88
A Drawing Book Alphabet 102
"The Duck and the Kangaroo" 11
Durrell, Lawrence 76, 103

"Eclogue" 91-94
Ede, Lisa 29, 43-44, 112
Edward Lear in Corsica: The Journal of a Landscape Painter 103
Edward Lear in Greece 103
Edward Lear in Southern Italy 103
Edward Lear in the Levant: Travels in Albania, Greece and Turkey in Europe: 1848-1849 81, 103, 113
Edward Lear's Indian Journal: Watercolours and Extracts from the Diary of Edward Lear (1873-1875) 79-80, 103
Edward Lear's Journals: A Selection 79, 103
Edward Lear: Selected Letters 103, 113
Edward Lear: The Corfu Years: A Chronicle Presented through his Letters and Journals 81, 103, 113
Edward Lear: The Cretan Journal 81, 103, 111

Ehrenpreis, Anne Henry 70-71, 110
Eliot, T. S. 9
Encyclopedia Britannica 85, 105
Enzensberger, Hans Magnus 21, 110
The Examiner 3, 5, 104
Eyton, Thomas Campbell 100

Facsimile of a Nonsense Alphabet Drawn and Written by Edward Lear 101
The Field of Nonsense 13
Fischer, Grete 16, 108
For Lovers of Birds 102
For Lovers of Cats 102
For Lovers of Flowers and Gardens 102
For Lovers of Food 102
Fortescue, Chichester 73-74, 89
Fortnightly Review 106
Fowler, Rowena 80-81, 103, 111
Fox, Geoff 110

Gallup, Donald C. 94-95, 102, 112
The Gardens and Menagerie of the Zoological Society Delineated 99
The Genera of Birds 113
Genre 113
Gerhard, Roberto 72
Glasgow, Eric 82, 111
Gleanings from the Menagerie and Aviary at Knowsley Hall 50, 99
Gorey, Edward 26
Gould, Elizabeth 53
Gould, John 46, 53, 99-100
Grassi, Aldo Vittorio 28, 112
Gray, Donald J. 41, 108
Gray, George Robert 100
Gray, John Edward 50, 99-100
Greene, David L. 21, 110
Grinke, Paul 60
Gross, Miriam T. 113

Hale, Susan 26
Hammond, Graham 110
Hardie, Martin 56, 105
Hark, Ina Rae 21-24, 27, 30, 64, 88, 110-11, 113
Harmon, William 26, 111
Harvard Library Bulletin 110
Hearn, Michael Patrick 54, 67, 112
Hildebrandt, Rolf 39, 107
Hill, Rosemary 68, 111

A History of Quadrupeds, including the Cetacea 46
The History of Sixteen Wonderful Old Women 25-26
A History of the Testudinata 99
Hofer, Philip 51, 57, 61, 63, 70 86, 94, 101, 107-8
Hogg, James 111
"How Pleasant To Know Mr. Lear" 91
Hunt, William Holman 47-48, 58, 62-63, 67-68
Huxley, Aldous 12, 105
Hyman, Susan 46, 52-53, 82, 103, 110, 113

Icones Avium 100
Illustrated Excursions in Italy 77-78, 80, 101
Illustrations of British Ornothology 46, 99
Illustrations of the Duck Tribe 100
Illustrations of the Family of Psittacidae, or Parrots 46, 49, 52, 54, 99
Impossible Picturesqueness: Edward Lear's Indian Watercolours 1873-1875 103, 106
"Incidents in the Life of My Uncle Arly" 4, 91

Jackson, Holbrook 14-15, 101, 106
Jackson, C. E. 50-51, 109
Jardine, Sir William 46, 49, 99-100
Jenkyns, Richard 88, 113
Jerrold, Walter 7-8, 74-75, 105
The Journal of Pre-Raphaelite Studies 111
The Journal of the Lewis Carroll Society 110
Journal of the Royal Institute of British Architects 57, 106
Journals of a Landscape Painter in Corsica 77, 80, 82, 101
Journals of a Landscape Painter in Greece and Albania, &c 77-80, 101
Journals of a Landscape Painter in Southern Calabria and the Kingdom of Naples 77-80, 101
Joyce, James 18, 26, 45
Judy, or the London Serio-Comic Journal 3, 104
"The Jumblies" 11

Kastner, John 54, 111
Kastner, Joseph 113
Kelen, Emery 87, 109
Kent, Muriel 9, 106
Kerr, Lord Ralph 100
Kipling, Rudyard 26
Kokali, Giorgio 89

Lambourne, Maureen 53-54, 108, 111
Lancaster, Sir Osbert 63-64
Later Letters of Edward Lear 103
Laughable Lyrics 4, 14, 101, 104
Lear, Ann 88
Lear Alphabet ABC 102
The Lear Coloured Bird Book for Children 101
Lear in Sicily 103
Lear in the Original 102
The Lear Omnibus 101
Lear's Corfu: An Anthology Drawn from the Painter's Letters 103
Legman, Gershon 25, 107
Lehmann, John 19-20, 55, 63, 88, 110
Leimert, Erika 37-38, 106
Letters of Edward Lear to Chichester Fortescue and Frances Countess Waldegrave 102-3, 105
Lewsen, Charles 102
Liebert, Herman W. 18-19, 23, 102, 109
Liede, Alfred 40, 107
Lister, Raymond 68, 113
Literary Onomastics Studies 27, 112
Lorrain, Claude 67-68
Lushington, Franklin 55, 78, 82, 85-86, 89, 105
Lyons, Ann Kearns 23
Lyons, Thomas R. 23

Maas, Jeremy 49, 51, 62-63, 66-67, 109, 111
Macmillan's Magazine 78, 105
Malcolm, Ian 56, 58, 105
Mallarmé, Stephane 9
Mangan, James Clarence 26
Mégroz, R. L. 10-13, 58, 75, 101, 106
Miller, Edmund 18, 109
Mills, Spencer 80
Mokrovols'kyi, O. 28
A Monograph of the Trogonidae, or Family of Trogons 100

A Monograph of the Ramphastidae, or Family of Toucans 46, 99
A Monograph on the Anatidae, or Duck Tribe 100
More Nonsense 3, 5-6, 14, 100
Morris, Edward 63, 110
Murphy, Ray 79-80
Murray, John 25, 78
Musical Opinion 110

The Nation 8
Natural History 112
The Naturalist's Library 100
Neuren Sprache 106
Neve, Christopher 53, 67-68, 80, 109, 112
New England Quarterly 82, 114
The New Statesman 108
New York Times Book Review 20
Nixon, Howard M. 15, 108
Noakes, Vivien 16-17, 22, 46, 48, 54-56, 62, 64, 66, 68-69, 75-78, 87, 102-3, 108, 112, 114
Nock, S. A. 11, 86, 106
Noel, F. M. 57
A Nonsense Alphabet 102
A Nonsense Birthday Book 101
Nonsense Books 101
Nonsense Drolleries 101
Nonsense Songs, Stones, Botany, and Alphabets 3, 4, 6, 14, 100
Nonsense Songs & Laughable Lyrics 101
Nonsense Songs and Stories 101
Northbrook, Earl of 7, 55

Ord, Priscilla A. 27, 112
Orwell, George 12-13, 23, 107
Osgood Field, William B. 57, 94, 106
The Owl and the Pussycat 100
"The Owl and the Pussycat" 11, 18, 21

The Pall Mall Magazine 4, 7, 104
Parisot, Henri 16, 109
Partridge, Eric 39, 107
"The Pelican" 70
"The Pelican Chorus" 11
Peterson, Roger Tory 51, 113
Petrassi, Goffredo 72
Petzold, Dieter 17, 40, 109
Pitman, Ruth 64-65

Plomer, William 55
"The Pobble Who Has No Toes" 12, 18
Poe, Edgar Allen 14
Poems of Alfred, Lord Tennyson 101
The Poetry of Nonsense 8, 36
Pollard, Arthur 23, 112
Pomè, P. 70
Prawer, S. S. 21, 110
Pre-Raphaelites 48, 58, 68
Preston, Michael J. 23
Prickett, Stephen 22, 110
Proby, Granville 79, 103
Proby, John Joshua 79

The Quarterly Review 3, 8, 33-34, 105
Queery Leary Nonsense: A Lear Nonsense Book 101
Quennell, Peter 88-89, 103, 107, 108

Reade, Brian 51-52, 59, 106
Reed, Langford 25, 105
Reichert, Klaus 40-41, 109
Rhymes of Nonsense: An Alphabet 102
Richardson, Joanna 16, 86, 108
Rieke, Alison 45, 82, 96, 114
Ritvo, Harriet 55, 112
Robinson, Fred Miller 90-91, 111
Rosa, Salvator 67
Rossetti, Dante Gabriel 11
Royal Academy of Arts 48, 54-55, 67
Runciman, Steven 66-67, 112
Ruskin, John 4-5, 9, 37, 67, 104

The Saturday Review 3-8, 84, 104-5
Schiller, Justin G. 27, 113
Seddon, Thomas 68
Selby, Prideaux John 99
Serra, Cristóbal 16, 108
Sewanee Review 11, 106
Sewell, Elizabeth 13-14, 18, 24, 38-39, 40-43, 107, 110
Sherrard, Philip 65, 81-82, 103, 113
Shipp, Horace 60, 108
Sitwell, Sir Sacheverell 50, 107
Slade, Bertha Coolidge 57
Smithsonian 111
The South Atlantic Quarterly 111
The Spectator 4-8, 34-35, 71, 104-5
St. Kiven and the Gentle Kathleen 102

Staley, Allen 65-66, 106
Stein, Gertrude 45
Stevens, Wallace 45, 82, 96
Stewart, Susan 42, 110
Strachey, Edmund 3, 6, 8, 34, 105
Strachey, Sir Edward 101, 105
Strachey, Henry 56-57, 61, 74, 105
Strachey, J. St. Loe 101
Strachey, Lady 7, 56, 74-75, 101, 102-3, 105
Stravinsky, Igor 72
The Studio 60, 107
Swainson, William 49
Swinburne, Algernon 9, 11

"The Table and the Chair" 11
Tait, Archbishop Campbell 71
Taylor, Richard 99
Taylor, Tom 56, 104
Teapots and Quails and Other New Nonsenses 102
Tennyson, Alfred 6, 9, 11, 33, 37, 48, 53, 65, 71, 78
Tennyson, Emily 47
Thompson, Randall 70-71, 108
Thomson, Virgil 72
"Three Receipts for Domestic Cooking" 12
Tigges, Wim 26-27, 43, 44-45, 112-13
Times 3, 105
Times Literary Supplement 21, 80, 87, 108-110, 115
Titian 67
Tortoises, Terrapins and Turtles 100
The Tragical Life and Death of Caius Marius Esq. 102
The Transactions of the Zoological Society 99
Tsigahov, Fari-Maria 82

Turner, J. M. 56, 61, 63, 65-67

Unicorn: An Independent Miscellaneous Journal 18, 109

van Leeuwen, Hendrik 29, 113
van Thal, Herbert 79, 103
The Victorian Newsletter 18, 109
Victorian Poetry 30, 110, 113-14
Victorian Studies 108
Views in Rome and its Environs 77-78, 100
Views in the Seven Ionian Islands 77-78, 101
Views in Seven Ionian Islands: A Facsimile of the Originial Edition Published in 1863 by the Artist 103
Vigors, N. A. 49

Waldegrave, Lady Frances Countess 7, 62, 74
Wales, H R H The Prince of 68
Westergaard, Peter 72
Whittet, G. S. 60, 107
Whorf, Benjamin 43
Willis, Gary 24-25, 110

The Yale University Library Gazette 94, 112
Ye Long Nite in ye Wonderfull Bedde 102

The Zoology of Captain Beechey's Voyage 100
The Zoology of the Voyage of the HMS Beagle 100
Zukofsky, Louis 45